EARLY BUDDHIST ARCHITECTURE

Japanese Arts Library

General Editor
John Rosenfield

With the cooperation and under the editorial supervision of:

The Agency for Cultural Affairs of the Japanese Government
Tokyo National Museum
Kyoto National Museum
Nara National Museum

KODANSHA INTERNATIONAL LTD. AND SHIBUNDO
Tokyo, New York, and San Francisco

Early Buddhist Architecture
in Japan

Kakichi Suzuki

translated and adapted by

Mary Neighbour Parent
and
Nancy Shatzman Steinhardt

Publication of this book was assisted by a grant from the Japan Foundation.

Early Buddhist Architecture in Japan was originally published in Japanese by the Shibundo publishing company, Tokyo, in 1971, under the title *Jōdai no jiin kenchiku*, as volume 65 in the series *Nihon no bijutsu*. The English edition was prepared at Kodansha International, Tokyo, by Saburo Nobuki, Takako Suzuki, and Michael Brase.

Distributed in the United States by Kodansha International/USA Ltd., through Harper & Row Publishers, Inc., 10 East 53rd Street, New York, New York 10022; in Europe by Boxerbooks Inc., Limmatstrasse 111, 8031 Zurich; and in Japan by Kodansha International Ltd., 2-12-21 Otowa, Bunkyo-ku, Tokyo 112.

Published by Kodansha International Ltd., 2-12-21 Otowa, Bunkyo-ku, Tokyo 112 and Kodansha International/USA Ltd., 10 East 53rd Street, New York, New York 10022 and 44 Montgomery Street, San Francisco, California 94104. Copyright © 1980 by Kodansha International Ltd. and Shibundo. All rights reserved. Printed in Japan.

Suzuki, Kakichi, 1928-
 Early Buddhist architecture in Japan.

 (Japanese arts library; 9)
 Translation of Jōdai no jiin kenchiku.
 Bibliography: p.
 Includes index.
 1. Temples, Buddhist—Japan. 2. Temples—Japan.
3. Architecture—Japan—To 794. 4. Architecture—
Japan—Heian period, 794–1185. 5. Ise Daijingū.
 I. Title. II. Series.
NA6053.2.S8913 726′.1′43920952 79–7342
ISBN 0-87011-386-0

First edition, 1980

CONTENTS

1. East pagoda, Yakushi-ji.
The east pagoda of the Yakushi-ji monastery is a masterpiece of early Buddhist architecture in Japan. Surviving with only minor repairs, it is thought to preserve the style of the late seventh century. Its most remarkable feature is the *mokoshi*, a lean-to type component attached to each of the three levels so that from a distance the pagoda appears to consist of six stories. Through the *mokoshi* and the nine-ringed finial topped by a decorative ornament, the pagoda achieves a superb balance; the verticality of the tall thin structure is offset by the strong horizontal force which cuts across it. In beauty of form, the east pagoda is the crowning glory of early Japanese architecture.

Japanese Art Periods

Prehistoric		–537
Asuka		538–644
Nara		645–781
Hakuhō	645–710	
Tempyō	711–781	
Heian		782–1184
Jōgan	782–897	
Fujiwara	898–1184	
Kamakura		1185–1332
Nambokuchō		1333–91
Muromachi		1392–1572
Momoyama		1573–99
Edo		1600–1867

Note: This table, compiled by the Agency for Cultural Affairs of the Japanese Government for the arts and crafts, has been adopted for general use in this series. In this volume, however, the dates of historical periods have been determined by the author and are slightly different from those above.

A Note to the Reader

Japanese names are given in the customary Japanese order, surname preceding given name. The names of temples and subordinate buildings can be discerned by their suffixes: *-ji*, *-tera*, *-dera* referring to temples (Tōshōdai-ji; Ishiyama-dera); *-in* usually to a subtemple attached to a temple (Shōryō-in at Hōryū-ji), not to be confused with the *-in* which refers to a certain precinct of the monastery, as in *tōin* or east precinct; *-dō* to a building with a special function (*jikidō*, or refectory); *bō* to a monastic residence (Gokuraku-bō).

ILLUSTRATIONS

INTRODUCTION

Among the arts of the world, one that has been sorely neglected by Western scholars is the traditional architecture of Japan. To be sure, in recent years short accounts of a very general nature, or poetic essays illustrated with magnificent photographs, have occasionally appeared, but scholarly treatments of accurately detailed structural methods are almost nonexistent. Consequently, this concise account of Japanese ancient Buddhist temple architecture, which was originally written for the general Japanese reader, is an important step toward meeting the dire need for material on Japanese architectural history in the English language. Moreover, the fact that this book deals with the first historical period of Japanese architectural development makes it the logical starting point for those who wish to study the architecture of later periods.

Since all the traditional Buddhist architecture of Japan looks similar to the un-initiated, the reader may wonder why the author chose to limit this book to a discussion of the ancient era. There are several reasons. First, the history of Japan is broadly divided into four epochs, the ancient (593–1184), the medieval (1185–1572), the recent (1573–1867), and the modern (1868 to the present). Major changes in every field, including the history of architecture, allow such divisions. Since the history of Japanese architecture is a complicated one, it would be impossible in one volume to treat the entire range of development and change in sufficient detail. Secondly, the foundation of all later traditional architecture up to the modern period was firmly established during the ancient period. Therefore, a knowledge of ancient architecture is necessary to a study of the architecture of the medieval or recent ages. The modern age dawned with Japan opening to the Western world, bringing with it totally new methods and materials for construction and drawing the country into the international stream of architectural expression.

It might be noted here that each of the broad historical divisions mentioned above can be further divided into shorter time spans. The ancient epoch, the period covered by this book, includes the Asuka (593–661), Nara (662–781), and Heian (782–1184) periods. The Nara period is often divided further into the early Nara or Hakuhō period (662–710) and the late Nara or Tempyō period (711–781). These periods are discussed in the Glossary.

13

It is reasonable to ask why the author treats only Buddhist architecture. The answer is unfortunately simple. There are no other extant buildings to be studied. It is, therefore, only through a study of Buddhist temple architecture that any continuity of the ancient architectural development can be ascertained. Of other extant buildings, the oldest can be dated only to the end of the Heian period.

The historical period in Japan begins with the official introduction of Buddhism from Korea, namely, the Paekche kingdom, in the middle of the sixth century. Since Japan's close contacts with Korea date from at least as early as the fourth century A.D., it follows naturally that Chinese civilization, to which the Korean peninsula had long been exposed, would be introduced from there. This is particularly so since China was politically unstable during the fourth, fifth, and sixth centuries, discouraging important direct communication. Japan had undoubtedly been exposed to Buddhism as well as the written Chinese language before they were officially introduced to the island country. The Japanese, however, were too preoccupied with establishing a foothold on the Korean peninsula to be interested in the potential of a written language beyond what would be needed by scribes in keeping accounts. Thus these centuries can only be described as a period of protohistory, the architecture of which consisted of lightly constructed shelters of the simplest type.

That there was no desire for solid, permanent structures is indicated by the fact that upon the demise of an emperor, his seat of government was abandoned, and his successor built anew in another place not contaminated by death. These events are set down in two lengthy chronologies at the beginning of the eighth century, long after most of the events had taken place. Even between the official introduction of Buddhism in the middle of the sixth century and the move to the newly constructed capital of Heijō in Nara at the beginning of the eighth century, there had been several capitals, including Naniwa (part of present-day Osaka), Ōtsu (in Shiga Prefecture), Asuka (in Nara Prefecture), and the Fujiwara capital (in Nara Prefecture). The capital at Fujiwara, although intended to be permanent, was soon found to be too small, necessitating the establishment of a much larger site at Heijō. Heijō was laid out in an orderly grid pattern similar to but smaller than Ch'ang-an (Sian), capital of the Chinese T'ang dynasty (A.D. 618-ca. 907), which served as its model. Today, there is nothing left of these imperial centers except what the archaeologist's spade has unearthed. In the case of Heijō, where extensive excavations have been completed, a wealth of valuable material has come to light. For our study, most important are the foundation stones, the roof tiles, and bits of decayed wooden building parts. Not only Heijō, but Asuka, Fujiwara, and many other sites that have been excavated, both in Nara Prefecture and elsewhere, have all revealed valuable clues to the arrangement and size of various buildings, from which can be deduced the probable structural system. But since no structure remains from the Asuka period (593–661), all descriptions of Asuka buildings other than those of their foundations are based on supposition.

In spite of the severe factional strife surrounding the new foreign religion of Buddhism at its inception, by the latter part of the sixth century it was well entrenched. The last two decades of the century saw the completion of two great temples, Shitennō-ji at Naniwa (now in present-day Osaka) and Asuka-dera (also called Hōkō-ji), located in the present village of Asuka in Nara Prefecture. Shitennō-ji was destroyed and rebuilt many times, the latest reconstruction taking place after the temple had been reduced to rubble during World War II. Rebuilt on its old foundations after the site had been excavated, the new reconstruction makes use of reinforced concrete to simulate the ancient wooden forms. At Asuka-dera, the original buildings were burned down in the Kamakura period (1185–1330) and never rebuilt. The site was excavated in 1956–57 and much valuable data regarding the earliest period of Buddhist architecture was uncovered. To be sure, there are many unclear points remaining, but the arrangement of individual buildings, their proximity to each other, and their plans and sizes have become clear. Roof tiles with patterns closely resembling those found at sites of the ancient Paekche kingdom support the assumption that the earliest temples were probably extremely similar to those of that kingdom.

Although there are no extant buildings from the Asuka period, and although we lack much knowledge and material from which to evaluate its architecture, it can be affirmed that it was a period of concentrated learning of new methods and new forms of building, a time of imitation and absorption. From the early Nara period through the late, there was also direct influence from China resulting in further avid imitation, but at the same time the Japanese had developed enough confidence in their mastery of building techniques to allow them to undertake temple construction without depending on their foreign teachers. Their natural tendency to selectivity gradually took precedence over total imitation, and by the mid-eighth century a religious architecture of classic proportions took shape, one that, though certainly utilizing Chinese methods, reflected the preferences for subtlety and refinement of form so characteristically Japanese. The Heian period saw a further Japanization of architectural forms and a new inventiveness, as intercourse with China, enjoyed from the seventh century on, was curtailed and finally cut off due to the decline and fall of the T'ang dynasty (618-ca. 907). Dr. Kakichi Suzuki gives a clear account of this process through his handling of the most important extant structures from Hōryū-ji in the late seventh century to the mid-twelfth-century rebuilding of the Taima-dera Mandara-dō (hondō, or main hall).

Before going further, it is best to clarify the use of the words "temple" and "monastery." In this book, they are used more or less synonymously since the distinction between them is not as clear as that between church and monastery in Christendom. If any difference is perceived, it would be in regard to the great official religious centers

15

housing large numbers of monks and providing study centers wherein devotees of different sects could peruse and expound on the sutras (the sacred writings of Buddhism) of their particular orientation. In the ancient period, no hard and fast boundaries separated the sects. Monks of all ranks, from those performing the menial tasks to the head priests, lived out their lives in apparent harmony. Within a huge compound were a number of subsidiary precincts with their buildings dedicated to the worship of a particular deity. Such large religious institutions can be thought of as monasteries. On the other hand, the word "temple" can apply to either the arrangement described above or to a very small place of worship that includes only a main image hall and living quarters for two or three priests.

There is also the word "shrine." To avoid confusion, this word is customarily applied to those compounds or individual buildings devoted to Shinto ("The Way of the Gods"), the indigenous animistic religion of Japan. An exception is the miniature Tamamushi Shrine owned by Hōryū-ji. It houses a small Kannon statue and is decorated with paintings illustrating the Buddha throwing himself to a lioness, to be devoured in place of her cubs.

Next we should perhaps examine the kinds of buildings that composed a temple. From the end of the sixth century to the end of the eighth century, the pagoda was the focal point of the temple. It was a multistoried towerlike structure in which were preserved the hallowed Buddhist relics. The pagoda is marked by a roof crowned with a metal finial (*sōrin*) usually made of bronze (pl. 2). The finial has a square base (*roban*) over which is a small dome that looks like an inverted bowl (*fukubachi*), with lotus petals (*ukebana*) placed on top. Around the central shaft are usually nine metal

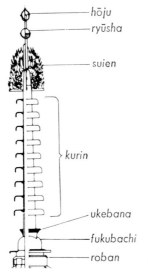

hōju
ryūsha

suien

kurin

ukebana
fukubachi
roban

2. Pagoda finial.

16

rings (*kurin*). Above this is a filigreed metal ornament (*suien*) extending at right angles to the shaft in four directions. On the shaft above is first a spherical shape (*ryūsha*) and at the very top a bulbous-shaped form (*hōju*) symbolizing the sacred jewel.

Next in importance was the image hall, called the *kondō* or *hondō*. The origin of the former name, which literally means "golden hall," can probably be ascribed to the gilded images contained therein, while the latter name, *hondō*, meaning "main hall," was perhaps first used when the images were no longer gilded and the pagoda was relegated to a place of secondary importance. "Buddha hall" (*butsuden* or *butsudō*) is a general term, during the ancient period, for buildings that house the image of a Buddha, bodhisattva, or other sacred figure.

The pagoda and *kondō* formed the nucleus or sacred precinct of the temple and were enclosed by a roofed corridor (*kairō*), opened on its inner side and closed by a wall and slat windows (*renji mado*) on its outer side; thus, it can be called a semienclosed roofed corridor (pl. 43). It was attached to either side of the middle gate (*chūmon*), extending for some distance until it changed direction at a 90° angle, continued up the sides and turned again at the rear of the sacred precinct, running until it was again attached to another building, sometimes a lecture hall, sometimes a second *kondō*. In some arrangements there was no interruption, only the corridor across the entire rear of the precinct (pls. 23, 31).

The middle gate traditionally faced south as did the main gate (*nandaimon*, "great south gate") that was placed some distance beyond the middle gate on the boundary of the entire temple compound. Depending upon the size of the area, one or two gates opened in the side and rear walls (pl. 64).

Because the temple compounds housed large numbers of monks and priests, living quarters (*sōbō*) and refectories (*jikidō*) were essential, and were placed outside the sacred precinct. There is still much that is unclear or completely unknown regarding the exact placement of these buildings.

The monks had to receive instruction. Therefore a lecture hall (*kōdō*) was necessary. It is a possibility that the lecture hall may also have served as a refectory in some temples. A repository constructed to house the sutras, the sacred writing from which the priests explained doctrine or both priests and monks chanted their liturgy, is called a sutra repository (*kyōzō*). Storehouses for precious objects or simply for safeguarding the resources of the temple are known by several names in Japanese, one of which is *shōsō*, the most famous and familiar example being the Shōsō-in of Tōdai-ji in Nara. All the extant storehouses of this type except the Kōfū-zō of Hōryū-ji were built of logs, triangular in section with their edges planed off so that they could fit together easily. This type of log storehouse is called an *azekura*.

A belfry (*shurō* or *shōrō*), a small building similar to the sutra repository, was usually placed opposite it, and both were located outside the sacred precinct. Administrative offices (*mandokoro*) were also included, but to what extent they were housed in separate buildings or shared space in some other building is not clearly known.

Throughout the seventh and eighth centuries, Buddhism gained the support of more and more members of the imperial family; empresses and emperors alike spent enormous sums for the support of the great temples, above all for Tōdai-ji. It became a custom to erect many smaller buildings within the boundaries of the temple, set apart and surrounded by semienclosed roofed corridors or high walls. Such areas are considered separate precincts (*betsu-in*), but they were not independent of the main temple. Subsidiary precincts might contain a pagoda, an octagonal hall dedicated to a particular deity, or even a pagoda and a *kondō*. Again caution is needed because there is still much excavation of subsidiary precincts that must be undertaken, and it can be hoped that such investigation will unearth new valuable information. The foregoing describes the buildings which are quite easily identified from excavated foundation stones, but many have been brought to light that are not as yet identified.

The arrangement of the buildings were based on two plans. The one in which the pagoda, *kondō*, and lecture hall were on the same axis as the great south and middle gates is known as the Shitennō-ji plan (pl. 31). The other is the Hōryū-ji plan, in which pagoda and *kondō* are no longer on the main axis but instead juxtaposed on either side of it (pl. 36). There were several variations of these plans. The Shitennō-ji plan was clearly introduced from the Paekche kingdom, which had in turn received it from China. The Hōryū-ji plan can be considered a Japanese innovation as there is no evidence to date that such an arrangement was ever used in China or Korea. After the beginning of the eighth century, with new influences from China, the pagodas, though doubled, were placed outside and in front of the sacred precinct; this was a step toward reducing the importance of the pagoda, a trend which continued until by the end of the century the pagoda was relegated to an insignificant place often away from the mainstream of temple activity. In the ninth century, with the introduction of the new Esoteric Buddhist sects, Shingon and Tendai, which preferred to locate their temples deep in the mountains, the entire arrangement of buildings became irregular, as dictated by the terrain. Many new types of halls were also required by the Esoteric sects. There were halls dedicated to individual deities, for example, Dainichi, and hence a *dainichidō* was required. Others included those housing a group of deities (*godaidō*), purification halls (*kanjōdō*), ordination halls (*kaidan'in*), halls for meditating while circumambulating (*jōgyō-sammaidō*) or for some special observance like that held on ten days of the month according to the lunar calendar (*jissaidō*).

Another sect which grew to great popularity during the Heian period was the Pure Land sect, with the Amida Buddha at its center. Thus, Amida halls (*amidadō*) were built to house images of Amida, the benevolent ruler of the Western Paradise. To avoid confusion, it must be understood that, as in the earlier periods, one temple could include more than one sect; for example, Enryaku-ji (in Shiga Prefecture), primarily a temple of Esoteric Tendai Buddhism, also was a supporter of Amidism.

Multistoried pagodas (pl. 1) continued to be built but no longer held the focal point. In addition to or in place of this type was a new kind, the single-storied *hōtō* or *tahōtō*, preferred by Esoteric Buddhism (pl. 128). It is thought that originally these resembled the Indian stupa much more closely than the multistoried type, which had undergone profound changes in its long journey from India to China. Probably at first it was only a cylindrical form rounded over the top and covered with layers of mud plaster, the final coat producing a smooth white finish. Perhaps it had no special roof and was only crowned with some kind of finial similar to that of the usual pagoda. But the frequent heavy rains in Japan would have quickly damaged it, thus requiring the addition of a protective roof. Sometimes a *mokoshi* (an enclosure with a pent roof) was added to safeguard the lower part and, incidentally, to create more interior space. The structural aspects of a *mokoshi* will be explained a little bit further on. No *tahōtō* is extant from the Heian period, but the oldest in existence is dated 1194, only nine years after the end of this period, too soon to have developed any characteristics distinguishing it as a building of a new age; it can thus be presumed to furnish us with a fairly accurate view of what the Heian-style *tahōtō* was like, even though it has undergone frequent repairs.

Let us now turn to the basic aspects of construction. If we seek points in common between traditional Japanese architecture and that of the Western world, we may be at the same time disappointed and challenged, for there are relatively few similarities. Certain fundamental building shapes, such as the rectangle, square, or octagon, are basic to both. Roof types, such as the gable and hipped, are also to be found in East and West. But the chief point in common is the use of the post-and-lintel system. Unlike Western architecture, in which the arch, systems of vaulting, and the truss have been widely used in addition to the post-and-lintel, traditional Japanese architecture is based exclusively on a post-and-lintel system strengthened by bearing blocks (*masu* or *to*) and bracket arms (*hijiki*) that extend out from the tops of the pillars (pl. 3).

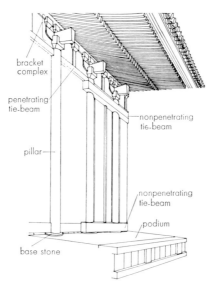

bracket complex

penetrating tie-beam

nonpenetrating tie-beam

pillar

nonpenetrating tie-beam

podium

base stone

3. Basic elements of temple architecture.

The post-and-lintel is fundamentally a very simple system composed of two up-rights and one crosspiece as the basic components, forming a unit that can be mul-tiplied indefinitely to extend the length of a building. However, the same is not the case in extending a post-free deep interior because a wooden beam is restricted by the length over which it can safely reach without further support. This problem under-lies the development of the complex support system characteristic of ancient East Asian architecture in general, and Japanese architecture in particular.

When we speak of Japanese traditional architecture, we are concerned with an architecture created primarily in wood. Large stands of various kinds of trees yielding excellent quality timber within a wide range of very hard to relatively soft woods provided a seemingly unlimited supply until recent times. On the other hand, because good building stone has always been scarce, it was used mainly for retaining walls and ancient tombs. Beyond a doubt, the nature of the available building material had a direct influence on the structural method employed. That Japan built in wood before the official advent of Buddhism in the mid-fifth century A.D. can be presumed, though no such early structures are extant. Pre-Buddhist buildings were undoubtedly of the simplest construction, like that seen today in the main sanctuary of the most important national shrine at Ise, which has been rebuilt almost every twenty years since the latter part of the seventh century (pl. 4). Important structural methods to note are posts set directly into the ground (*hottatebashira*) without any kind of base stone. These are connected by simple transverse beams that support center struts strengthened by diagonal braces (*sasu*) that normally carry the ridgepole (*munagi*). In the case of the Ise main sanctuary and a few other small shrine buildings else-where, the ridgepole is supported on pillars that stand free of the building on the gable sides. There is no curve in the thatched roof and no complex structural system supporting it. Furthermore, there was no necessity for anything more complicated, for the building is a very small three-by-two bays.

After Buddhism was introduced from the Paekche kingdom in southwest Korea, significant changes in building techniques took place. Although the structural method continued to be based on the post-and-lintel system, rectangular buildings increased in size so that a pillar or column* and the support system for the roof framework became a complex of bearing blocks and bracket arms. Elevated foundations or podia (*kidan*) were constructed of hard packed earth covered with a veneer of carefully dressed rectangular stone slabs or occasionally uncut stone (pl. 3). The lower part of the column was no longer placed directly into the earth but erected on a roughly circular stone base (*soseki*) set on top of the podium. Walls stretching between the col-umns were plastered, but in ancient buildings it was frequently done so that the

---

* A post can be thought of as a simple upright, square or circular; a pillar is more supportive, while a column, along with being supportive, also consists of a base and capital, or in the case of Japanese architecture, a bracket system in place of a capital. In this study, pillar and column are used inter-changeably.

4. Seiden, Inner Shrine, Ise Shrine. Sixtieth rebuilding, 1975.

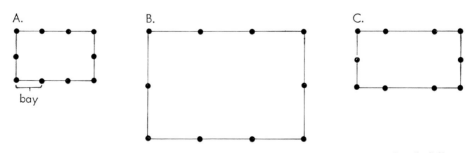

5. Plans of three-by-two-bay buildings.

intercolumnar structure was left visible. The roofing material on all important buildings became tile. Another influence from the continent was painting over the natural wood with red-orange, how bright or deep cannot be ascertained. The vertically slatted windows (*renji mado*) were painted green and the rafter ends yellow. In richly supported temples, the rafter ends were protected by a covering of metal with an openwork design like those of Hōryū-ji's pagoda and *kondō*. Although the Tōshōdai-ji *kondō* is the only ancient building still retaining on its ridge ends the curved forms called *shibi* (only the left one is original), they must have been common on most *kondō* (pl. 97). The miniature Tamamushi Shrine mentioned earlier also has them.

The plan of ancient temple buildings is relatively simple due to the limitation imposed by the post-and-lintel structural system. The length may vary considerably while the depth is restricted to the distance the transverse beams can stretch without additional support. Thus, there are no great or subtle variations in the basic plans. The upright supports for temple buildings are large, carefully formed cylindrical pillars (*hashira*), which are occasionally characterized by entasis, a slight convex curving of the shaft. The term "bay" (*ken*) designates the distance between two pillars and is measured from pillar center to pillar center. The plan of a building having, for example, three bays lengthwise and two bays in depth is written 3 × 2; the lengthwise direction is always given first. Moreover, the width of the bays may vary from building to building or even within the same building. For example, as can be seen in plate 5, all are three-by-two bays, yet the plan in plate 5b encloses a larger space. In plate 5c it can be seen that the center bay is wider than the lateral bays on either side of it. Buildings like these have columns only on the perimeter of the building. To extend their length is no problem because any number of bays can be added. The problem lies in increasing the depth. Again taking a three-by-two structure, if another row of pillars is added on one, two, three or all four sides, the building can be increased by one bay accordingly (pls. 6–7). The space created forms a kind of aisle, from here on called by the Japanese name, *hisashi*. The central space is the core of the building and is called the *moya*. It has been customary among Japanese carpenters and many scholars to describe a building in which *hisashi* have been added by giving the number of bays lengthwise in the *moya* plus the number of *hisashi* added. Thus "three bays, four sides" means a *moya* whose length is three bays with *hisashi* added around the entire *moya*. This has one unsatisfactory point: if the *moya* was three bays deep as sometimes was the case, such a description would not give this fact clearly. Thus, today, such a building will usually be described according to its overall number of lengthwise bays by the number of transverse bays. The previously described building would be five by four, presuming the *moya* to be two bays deep.

We now understand a building which has two concentric rectangles of columns. If the addition of *hisashi* front and back still did not result in a satisfactory depth, a further area could be created in front of the foremost *hisashi* by extending the roof and defining the area by yet another row of pillars. This new area is called the *mago-*

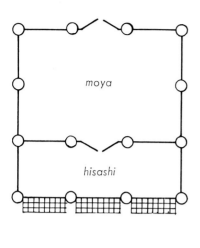

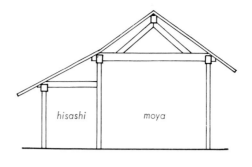

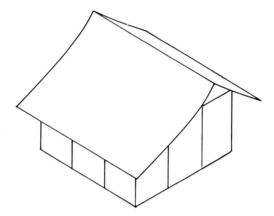

6. Building with *hisashi* on one side.

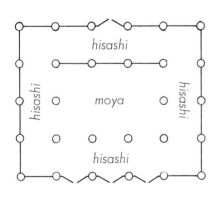

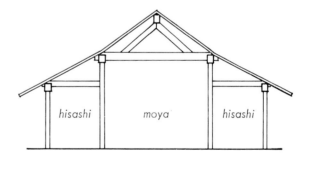

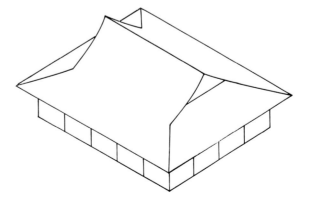

7. Building with *hisashi* on four sides.

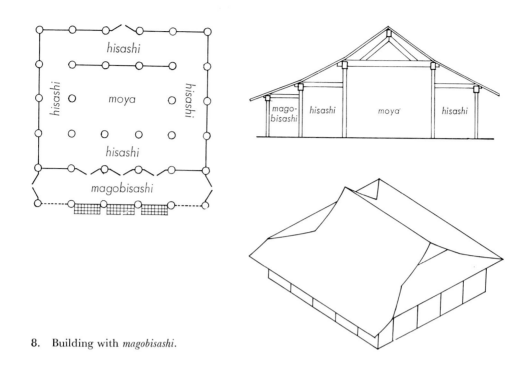

8. Building with *magobisashi*.

bisashi (pl. 8). This method was only fairly satisfactory because its roof tended to have too low a slope.

Another method used to increase the interior space was the addition of *mokoshi*, which were mentioned briefly in regard to the *tahōtō*. A *mokoshi* also forms another aisle either around the *moya* only, or it can be added to surround the *hisashi*. The difference between the *mokoshi* and *hisashi* is a structural one (pls. 9–10). The exterior row of pillars defining the *mokoshi*, like those bounding the *hisashi*, are usually lower than the pillars around the *moya* and are attached to the *moya* pillars by tie-beams. However, in the case of *hisashi*, bracket complexes are piled up above each of its pillars to bring them nearer the top of the *moya* pillars, which also have bracket complexes placed on top of them. The bracket complexes on the *moya* pillars all carry purlins to which the *moya* rafters coming from the ridge are joined, there meeting the rafters of the *hisashi* which stretch from the *moya* purlins to the wall purlins. A bend is formed where the *moya* rafters end and the *hisashi* begins. This bend is filled in with clay on which the tiles are laid. Thus a curve is created on the roof surface, but the contour of the roof forms one continuous line. On the other hand, in the case of a *mokoshi*, the exterior line of pillars is tied to the shafts of either the *hisashi* or *moya* pillars, depending on the building, and then rafters are laid from beams attached to the inner line of pillars to the purlins set above the outer row of pillars that define the *mokoshi*. The result is a pent roof separated from, and lying below, the main roof. The building looks like a two-storied structure from the exterior, but it is really only one story. The Hōryū-ji *kondō*, however, is a true two-storied structure that has a separately roofed *moya*; the *hisashi* rafters extend from a superstructure erected above the *moya* pillars and are supported by wall and eave purlins (pl. 39).

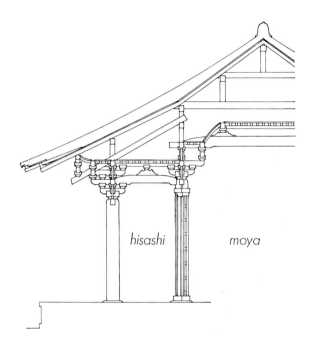

9. Structure and overall view of building with *hisashi*.

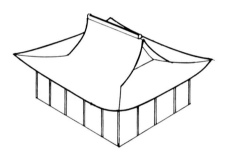

hisashi   *moya*

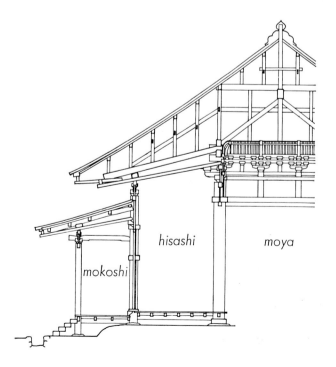

10. Structure and overall view of building with *hisashi* and *mokoshi*.

hisashi   *moya*

mokoshi

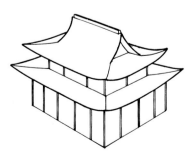

25

A *mokoshi* with a nearly flat roof and short slender pillars has been added beyond the *hisashi*. It is a subject for debate whether this *mokoshi* was part of the original *kondō* or added at some later date.

It was convenient to distinguish between the pillars surrounding the *moya* and those of the *hisashi*. The former were logically called interior or inside pillars (*irigawabashira*), or we could simply say *moya* pillars, and those of the *hisashi*, because they were usually on the outside wall of the building, were named exterior or outside pillars (*gawabashira*). These we could call *hisashi* pillars.

Purlins (*keta*) are beams which run the length of the building and are placed either directly on the top of the pillars in the simplest construction or are held by bearing blocks joined to bracket arms. Those on top of the pillars of the exterior wall are called wall purlins (*gawageta*); those on top of the interior row of pillars surrounding the *moya* are called either *moya* purlins (*moyageta*) or simply inside purlins (*irigawageta*). Purlins are also used above struts to form the roof framework. Those above the *moya* may also be called purlins or *moya* purlins.

Transverse beams or crossbeams (*hari*) are beams that span the depth of the building. The ridge or ridgepole (*mune* or *munagi*) is a long beam running the length of the building at the very top of the framework, forming a junction where the two inclined roof surfaces meet. Between the ridges and the lowest transverse beams, a roof support system consisting of struts (*tsuka*) and additional transverse beams was used in ancient temple buildings. There are two variations. One type consists of either a center strut (*munezuka*) to which diagonal braces (*sasu*) are attached, or simply diagonal alone (pl. 11). The center strut sometimes carries a bearing block which supports a beam (pl. 10). The second type is composed of two "rainbow" beams (*kōryō*) —that is, two transverse beams which are slightly curved and tapered on each end where they insert into bearing blocks on top of the *moya* pillars (pl. 12). "Frog-leg" struts (*kaerumata*) separate the lower rainbow beam from the one above it. These struts are so named because of their supposed resemblance to the legs of a crouching frog. They are placed about a quarter distance in from each end of the rainbow beam. Bearing blocks attached to the tops of these decorative struts form a support for the purlins over the *moya* and for a second rainbow beam that has one frog-leg strut positioned in its center to carry the ridgepole. This structure is called a double rainbow beam with frog-leg struts (*nijū kōryō kaerumata*). If the roof framework is hidden by a ceiling as it is in the monks' dormitory at Gangō-ji (restoration), there is no need for decorative rainbow beams and frog-leg struts. Instead, double transverse beams (*nijūbari*) separated by ordinary struts are used (pl. 13). In ancient buildings with double rainbow beams and frog-leg struts used over the *moya*, a single penetrating rainbow tie-beam was commonly used in the *hisashi* to join the *hisashi* pillars to the *moya* pillars. Upon completion of this framework, common base rafters are set and sheathing of board or perhaps roped lath is laid on the rafters to make a base on which to spread the clay that receives the roof tiles.

It is well to say a word about rafters (*taruki*). We have already mentioned the common base rafters (*jidaruki*). In the ancient period rafters are often round in section, but square or somewhat rectangular base rafters gradually supersede their use. A separate short rafter attached to and extending out beyond the base rafter at a different angle is called a "flying" rafter (*hiendaruki*; pl. 14). This rafter is never circular in

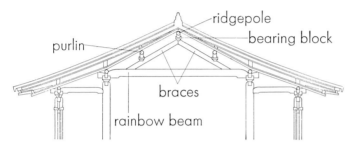

11.   Roof with diagonal braces.

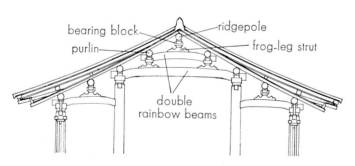

12.   Roof with double rainbow beams and frog-leg struts.

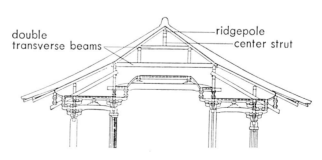

13.   Roof with double transverse beams.   27

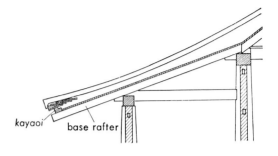

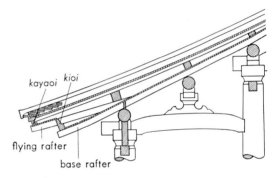

14. Single-eaved (above) and double-eaved (below) raftering.

section. To attach the flying rafters to the base rafters a long beam notched in a dentil pattern is laid across them from corner to corner, and the rear parts of the flying rafters are secured in the notches extending beyond to the inside, where their inner ends can be nailed to the base rafters. This member is called a flying rafter support (*kioi*). A further function of the flying rafter support is to raise the flying rafters so that their angle of incline is changed, thus preventing too much downward direction of the eaves. Another long curved horizontal member is laid across the tops of the flying rafters to support the eaves. This is called an eave support (*kayaoi*). Both the flying rafter support and the eave support greatly influence the extent to which the eaves curve up at the corners. When both base rafters and flying rafters form the eaves, it is expressed as double eaves (*futanoki*) in contrast to single eaves (*hitonoki*), in which flying rafters have been omitted and only base rafters form the eaves (pl. 14).

28

More about rafters: In ancient Japan, rafters were laid parallel with only one known exception, the remains of which were excavated at Shitennō-ji. Such parallel rafters are called *heikō-daruki* (pl. 15). When rafters are radiated at the corners or from a center point on each side of the building, they are called fan rafters (*ōgidaruki*). Such a system became popular after the introduction of two new styles of architecture introduced in the late twelfth and thirteenth centuries (Kamakura period) and are beyond the scope of this book. There are also rafters which are considerably larger than the common base or flying rafters. One kind are the "tail" rafters (*odaruki*) and the other are the hip rafters (*sumigi*). The former is a heavy rafter balanced like a fulcrum on either the bracket arm or a bearing block of the second step of a projecting bearing-block–bracket complex (*tokyō* or *kumimono*; pl. 17). This heavy, strongly slanted member both strengthens the bracket complex and supports the eave purlin

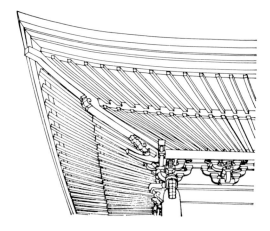

15. Fan (left; a medieval example) and parallel (below) raftering.

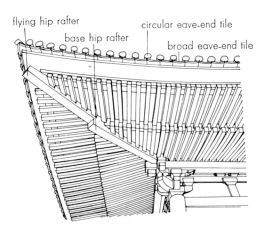

flying hip rafter

base hip rafter

circular eave-end tile

broad eave-end tile

29

(*degeta*). The hip rafter (*sumigi*) is used only in the hip roof or in the hipped part of a hip-and-gable roof. It is a heavy rafter used at the corner (pl. 15). In some buildings there are base hip rafters (*jisumigi*) and flying hip rafters (*hiensumigi*).

Two more rafter types must be mentioned: the exposed rafter (*keshōdaruki*) and the hidden rafter (*nodaruki*; pl. 16). In the late tenth century, a new roofing system was devised over the *hisashi* of the main lecture hall (Daikōdō) at Hōryū-ji. It consists of two layers of rafters separated by struts. The lower rafters are really the same as common base rafters, but since they are visible in contrast to the upper rafters concealed above them, they are now called exposed rafters (*keshōdaruki*) and the others are called hidden rafters (*nodaruki*). Before the end of the Heian period this technique was used to extend hidden rafters over the entire building resulting in a double-roof structure. The hidden rafters and the framework supporting them was called a hidden roof (*noyane*), and the exposed rafters and their supporting members combined to form an exposed roof (*keshōyane*). Such a system permitted the structure to be roofed at any chosen pitch independent of the lower part of the building. The exposed rafters could also be set at a gentle angle independent of the steeper incline of the hidden rafters. This new system created the necessity for a ceiling to hide the rough structure of the hidden roof.

We now come to the most complicated yet most characteristic feature of Japanese temple architecture, the system of bearing blocks and bracket arms (*tokyō* or *kumimono*), which are formed into complexes and set above the pillars. The simplest type is a

16.   The hidden roof system in area above *hisashi*, Daikōdō, Hōryū-ji.

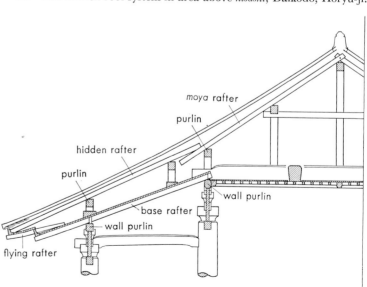

"boat-shaped" bracket (*funa-hijiki*) attached directly to the top of the pillar (pl. 17). However, sometimes a bearing block (*masu* or *to*) is placed on the top of the column first, and the boat-shaped bracket is added on top of this. As the complex is composed of one large bearing block (*daito*) and one bracket arm (*hijiki*), the two together are referred to as a large bearing block plus bracket arm or as a simple bracket complex (*daito-hijiki*). All parts of a bracket complex are joined by tenon and mortise. When bracket arms are inserted into the large bearing block only in the direction of the wall plane and three smaller bearing blocks (*makito*) are joined to them, the complex is called a three-on-one nonprojecting bracket complex (*hira-mitsudo*). In the Nara period, the top surface of the bracket arm that can be seen between the bearing blocks has a concave curve which gives it a scooped out appearance. This concave curve is called *sasaguri*, and it creates a pleasing curvilinear effect as it continues the curve of the bearing block. Later on, this concave curve is eliminated and the top surface is made straight across.

Bracket arms that are set not only parallel to the wall plane, but also at right angles to it and secured in the same large bearing block, constitute a three-on-one right-angle complex (*demitsudo*). Furthermore, such a bracket complex can be stepped out by adding another bracket arm and three small bearing blocks to the outermost bearing block at the end of the bracket arm which is at right angles to the wall. In this case the entire complex is called a one-stepped bracket complex (*degumi* or *hitote-saki*). By further addition of bearing blocks and brackets the complex may be extended twice, resulting in a two-stepped bracket complex (*futatesaki*); if three times, it becomes a three-stepped bracket complex (*mitesaki*) and so on. Four-stepped complexes (*yotesaki*) occur only on the *tahōtō*. The most popular type in Japan for important buildings was the three-stepped bracket complex. Added support for the eave purlin was necessary when the three-stepped bracket complex was used. This is provided by the tail rafter. It rests on the outermost bearing block of the second step of the bracket complex and on its end carries the third bracket complex that holds the eave purlin. Often the wall purlins need support between the bracket complexes. For this purpose, a strut capped with a bearing block (*kentozuka*) was used. The bearing block carried the wall purlin more firmly than if it rested only on top of the strut.

A small latticed ceiling (*noki-tenjō*) was installed under the eaves to hide the space between the eave purlin and the long bracket tie-beam (*tōshi-hijiki*; pl. 17). The Nara-period east pagoda at Yakushi-ji has a good example. The arrangement at the tenth-century five-storied pagoda at Daigo-ji in Kyoto has a narrow lattice ceiling stretching from the upper long bracket tie-beam to the purlin carried by the second step of the bracket arm and small bearing blocks; from this purlin to the eave purlin are convexly curved struts (*shirin*) that are not supporting members but act as a transition from the second step of the bracket complex to the third and also fill in what otherwise would be an ugly gap that would allow much dampness to penetrate under the eaves and above the bracket complexes.

17. Various types of bracket complexes.

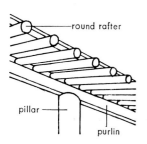

A. No bracket complex

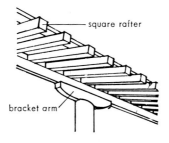

B. Boat-shaped bracket arm

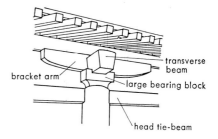

C. Simple bracket complex

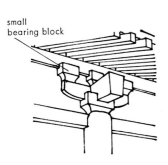

D. Three-on-one nonprojecting
    bracket complex

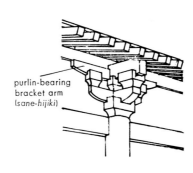

E. Three-on-one right-angle complex

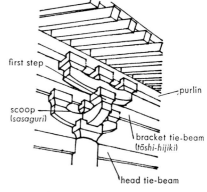

F. One-stepped bracket complex

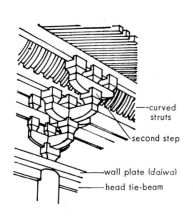

G. Two-stepped bracket complex

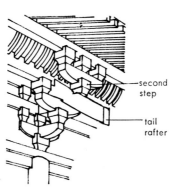

H. Two-stepped bracket complex
    with tail rafter

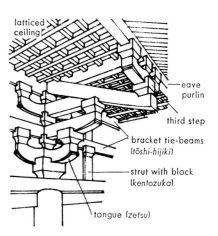

I. Three-stepped bracket complex

At the Hōryū-ji *kondō* and pagoda, at the Tamamushi Shrine, and at two neighboring three-story pagodas, a unique type of bracket complex can be seen. This type is called a "cloud-pattern" bracket (*kumo-hijiki*) and a "cloud-pattern" bearing block (*kumo-to*; pl. 18). They are unknown on the continent, which fact strongly supports the view that they were originated by the Japanese. They are decorative, suggesting a stylized cloud form. On their undersides they have a tonguelike or liplike form called a *zetsu*. These were added to the usual brackets at Yakushi-ji, but in later buildings they were eliminated. One more form peculiar to the Hōryū-ji *kondō* and pagoda is a flat platelike form (*saraita*) inserted between the large bearing block and the top of the pillar (pl. 18). Perhaps this plate was a carry-over of an Asuka-period technique into the Hakuhō period; it is not found in subsequent buildings until the Edo period (1615–1867), at which time the shape and proportion were changed.

18. Cloud-pattern bracket and bearing block.

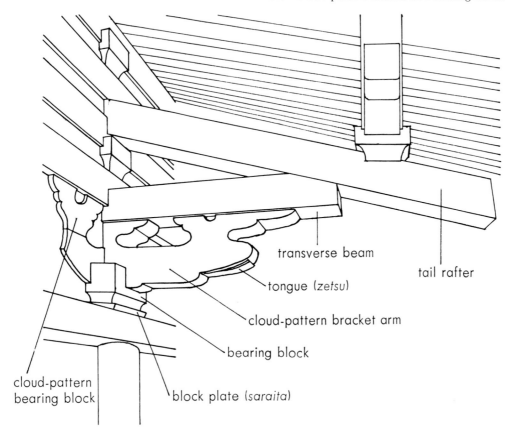

transverse beam

tail rafter

tongue (*zetsu*)

cloud-pattern bracket arm

bearing block

cloud-pattern bearing block

block plate (*saraita*)

33

With the heavy load carried on top of the pillars, it can be readily seen that some way had to be found to strengthen them. There were two methods. One was the use of "head" tie-beams (*kashira-nuki*), which were inserted into the tops of the pillars, tying them together securely (pl. 19). Another method was the use of horizontal timbers placed on the inside and outside of the pillars top and bottom. The inner surfaces of these members were hewed to fit the curve of the pillars. At the corners their outer surfaces met to form 90° angles. These are also a kind of tie-beam, and in the text we have called them nonpenetrating tie-beams (*nageshi*; pl. 3).

There was always the problem of increasing the depth of a building. One way, previously mentioned, was the addition of a *magobisashi*. Another method begun in the Nara period was the building of a twin structure used for a worship hall (*raidō*) in front of the main hall. If this structure was less deep than the one behind it, it was called a *hosodono*, meaning "narrow hall." Together these buildings were called twin halls (*narabidō*), and they were of the same length (pl. 20). With the invention of the hidden roof, two such structures could be combined under one huge roof.

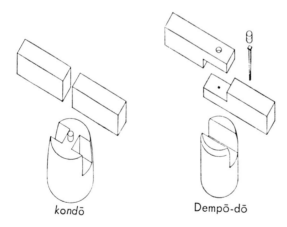

19. Four examples of head tie-beam joinery at Hōryū-ji (*kondō*, Asuka period; Dempō-dō, Tempyō period; belfry and Kōfū-zō, Heian period).

kondō

Dempō-dō

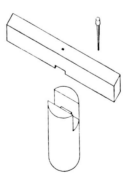

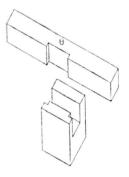

east precinct belfry

Kōfū-zō

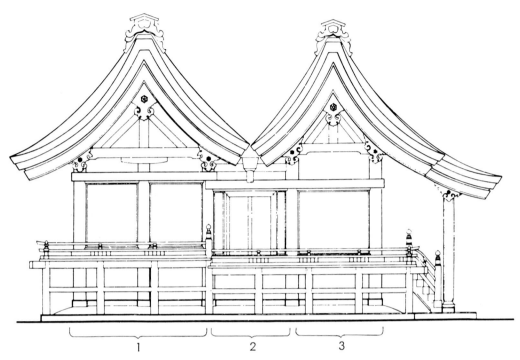

20. *Narabidō* (twin halls) as seen in shrine architecture (area #1 corresponding to the inner sanctuary, #2 to the *ai-no-ma* or point of juncture, #3 to the *raidō*). Main hall, Usa Hachiman Shrine, Ōita Prefecture.

What had been the separate worship hall or "narrow hall" now became an integral part of the main hall. The area holding the Buddhist altar and statues came to be called the inner sanctuary (*naijin*) while the area in front of it is called the outer sanctuary (*gejin*). In most cases the outer sanctuary can be considered the area for the laymen who come to pray and can be called either the *gejin* or the *raidō*.

It is hoped that this introduction will facilitate the reading of the many technical passages in Dr. Suzuki's book and that the reader, gaining insight into the complexities of ancient Japanese architectural history, will be motivated to continue into the volumes on the architecture of the middle ages, which will include shrines as well as temples, that are to be published as part of this series. Above all, it is hoped that the merit of Japanese traditional architecture will be understood, so that the West will see it in its rightful place beside the major architectural expressions of the world.

Mary Neighbour Parent   35

ACKNOWLEDGMENTS

Mrs. Steinhardt's translation of Dr. Kakichi Suzuki's book of 1971 was completed in the U.S.A. Dr. Parent, working in Japan with access to Professor Suzuki and other Japanese specialists, had the opportunity to consult primary archaeological and documentary material and to introduce into the manuscript more recent discoveries.

Nancy Shatzman Steinhardt: The assistance of specialists has been graciously given to me. My deepest debt of gratitude is to Tanaka Tan, of the Institute for Humanistic Studies of Kyoto University, for the many hours of discussion at his desk, for his explanatory drawings in correspondence, and for his patient initiation in how to look at a building. To him, to Huang Pao-yü of the College of Chinese Culture, Tai-pei, and to Ts'ai Mu-t'an of National Taiwan University, I offer my thanks for their painstaking explanations of both general and specialized problems in this book, and their constant encouragement. I would also like to thank Itasaka Gen of Harvard University for his elucidation of special problems and Japanese readings, and William H. Coaldrake, also of Harvard University, for his extensive revisions of technical terminology and meaning. No tribute of thanks or praise can adequately characterize John Rosenfield's involvement in this book. It was he who initiated, sponsored, and prodded it through every stage.

Mary Neighbour Parent: I wish to extend my deepest appreciation to my teachers, Dr. Eizō Inagaki and Dr. Kiyoshi Asano, who with incredible patience over the years have instructed me in this most difficult field. In regard to the translation of this book, they have always allowed me, no matter how busy they were, to interrupt them to make certain of many points about which I felt unsure. In addition, I wish to thank Associate Professor Hiroyuki Suzuki, in whose research room I have long held a desk, for his instant willingness to check any translation of which I felt doubtful. To the author, Dr. Kakichi Suzuki, I express my grateful appreciation for his lucid series of lectures given at the University of Tokyo in the spring of 1978. His explanations of structural aspects and his illustrations were of inestimable value in working on the translation of his book.

EARLY BUDDHIST ARCHITECTURE

1

THE INTRODUCTION
OF BUDDHIST ARCHITECTURE

THE ADVENT OF MAINLAND ARCHITECTURE

The transmission of Buddhism to Japan began with the presentation of a Buddha image and sutras by King Syŏng-myŏng of Paekche in the mid-sixth century A.D., fully one thousand years after the birth of the Buddha Śākyamuni. Shortly afterward, Buddha images were presented to Japan by the Korean kingdoms of Koguryŏ and Silla, and in 577 a temple master-carpenter, a tile maker, and an image maker, among others, sent by the Paekche king, arrived in the Yamato plain, the political center of Japan. Buddhism, transmitted to Japan in this way, became a cause of conflict between the Soga clan, supporters of the new religion, and the Mononobe and Naka-tomi families, who opposed it. In the year 585 an imperial edict was issued pro-hibiting the practice of Buddhism. The pretext of the prohibition was that Soga no Umako had begun building a Buddhist pagoda on Ōno Hill, and in the previous year had built a Buddhist hall at his private residence (the sites of both of these struc-tures are uncertain). In due course, the Soga family destroyed the opposing factions and, as if in testimony to his victory, Soga no Umako commenced construction in 588 of a monastery now called the Asuka-dera. For this task he invited a group of arti-sans from Paekche—two temple builders, four tile makers, a man to cast the bronze pagoda finial, and a painter—marking the first appearance of authentic mainland-style buildings in the Yamato region.

Advanced mainland architectural techniques had, in fact, come to Japan prior to this time. A fragment of a model clay house thought to date from about the fifth century shows the use of a basic element of the Chinese building system—a bearing block resting on a pillar (pl. 21). It was excavated at the Ishiyama tomb in Mie Prefecture. In the sixth century, Korean-style "mountain fortresses" (yamajiro) were built in the northern part of Kyushu (pl. 22). These fortresses are called kōgoishi, and according to an earlier theory were the boundaries of sacred compounds. To con-struct them, huge dressed stones were lined up side by side, and the soil was pounded layer on layer to form a high earthwork. At strategic points in the wall, gates and sluices were built, and it appears that military barracks and storehouses were estab-lished within. The system of granite construction used in the mountain fortresses and the rammed-earth techniques for building earthworks are linked to the techniques of

21. Clay house with incised drawing of pillar with large bearing block, fifth century. Excavated from Ishiyama tomb, Mie Prefecture. (Anonymous loan to Faculty of Letters, Kyoto University)

constructing the podia of Buddhist buildings; until this time these techniques were unknown to Japanese architecture, which secured the foundation by pillars set directly in the earth, without the use of base stones or earthworks. At present, however, we have found no evidence of the influence of mainland technology directly on architecture itself. Rather, in the northern Kyushu area there is a gap between the building of the mountain fortresses in the sixth century and the arrival of Buddhist architecture there somewhat late in the seventh.

We must keep in mind that architecture is different from sculpture and painting; it is an art that from the beginning is the product of the combination of many crafts, and for this reason the construction of buildings in a new style requires a successful synthesis of technical systems. Many naturalized Koreans were under the jurisdiction of the Soga clan, and it seems natural that they would have brought to Japan, little by little, the architectural techniques of their native Paekche or Koguryŏ. Soga no Umako's Buddha hall of Ishikawa and pagoda of Ōno Hill, neither of which has survived, must have been built with the skills of such immigrants. The Japanese, in all likelihood, were not satisfied with such improvisations and therefore summoned a group of craftsmen possessing the latest technology for the construction of the Asuka-dera. It was at this time that tile roofing first entered Japan, becoming so intimately

22. *Kōgoishi*, sixth century. Mount Kōra, Fukuoka Prefecture.

connected with temples that the expression *kawara-buki* (tile roof) became a common term of reference to indicate a temple. Furthermore, tradition says that a model *kondō* (main image hall of a monastery) was brought at this time, making it possible to build more faithfully in the continental architectural style.

A fourth-century description of the Chinese capital at Loyang (*Lo-yang ch'ieh-lan chi*) says that "the Hall of the Buddha is like the Throne Hall of State," implying that the styles of Chinese palaces and Buddhist temple architecture were similar. Buddhism is said to have entered China in the year A.D. 64 of the Later Han dynasty, and thus already had a long history there. During this time, whatever architectural forms had been introduced through Asia were completely transformed into the Chinese mode, and in regard to wooden architecture in particular, a unique Chinese style was developed. The form that the Chinese had developed for palace architecture was diverted just as it was to Buddhist purposes, indicating the extent to which Chinese architecture had progressed and become fully confident in its own resources. It is said that Buddhism was transmitted from China to the north Korean kingdom of Koguryŏ in 372, and to the southern kingdoms of Paekche and Silla in 384 and 528, respectively. Thus, together with the flow of Buddhism, Chinese architectural style passed through Korea and was transmitted to Japan.

41

THE DISTRIBUTION OF TEMPLE ARCHITECTURE

After the construction of the Asuka-dera at the very end of the sixth century, about the middle of the Asuka period (593–661), one by one other temples were erected. The buildings which best represent the early period are Prince Shōtoku's Shitennō-ji and Wakakusa-dera (the original Hōryū-ji); from the middle period is Kudaradai-ji from the reigns of the emperors Jomei (629–641) to Kōtoku (645–654); and following are Kawara-dera, Sūfuku-ji, and others of the Saimei (655–661) and Tenji (661–671) eras. These temples were all built under the patronage of the imperial family, but there were also clan temples from early times, built primarily by naturalized Japanese at first but later on a broader base, and the number of temples in Japan increased with great speed. The *Nihon shoki*, a history of Japan completed in 720, records forty-six Buddhist temples throughout the land by 625, but this figure seems to include establishments consisting of barely a single hall. As for complete monasteries, archaeological remains have revealed rather few.

At present, extant temple sites considered belonging to the early period are limited to the developed areas of the time, Yamato and Kawachi provinces (present-day Nara Prefecture and part of Osaka Prefecture), and their number hardly exceeds ten. Traces of Buddhist sanctuaries by the end of Asuka period (mid-seventh century) extend to northern Kyushu in the west and to western Aichi Prefecture in the east, and the total number is around fifty; in the countryside the number is exceedingly small. The majority of temples are concentrated in Nara Prefecture and part of Osaka Prefecture.

2

ASUKA-DERA AND KAWARA-DERA

Not one temple building survives from the Asuka period (593–661). The oldest extant structures were built after the middle of the seventh century, in the western precinct of Hōryū-ji. It was previously thought that the Hōryū-ji monastery employed the only Asuka-period style, but it has become clear since the Second World War that Asuka-period temple architecture was multistyled. This fact was revealed by excavations at the important temple sites of Asuka-dera, Shitennō-ji, and Kawara-dera.

Unique Building Remains

Asuka-dera was begun in the year 588 by workmen who had been summoned from Paekche to construct what became the first authentic Japanese Buddhist temple. The arrangement of the compound is different from the other temples of the period, having a pagoda in the center and *kondō* (main image halls) on three sides; no other example of this plan is known in Japan today (pl. 23). However, the excavated remains of the Ch'ongam-sa in Koguryǒ are very similar to it, so that Korean influence on Asuka-dera must have come not only from Paekche, but also from Koguryǒ in the north.

It is interesting to note that the roof tiles of nearby Toyura-dera, which seems to have been built at about the same time as Asuka-dera, are in the Koguryǒ manner (pl. 25), whereas those at Asuka-dera are of the Paekche mode (pls. 24, 26–27). Thus, from the very beginning of Buddhist architecture in Japan there was a mixture of two styles. Even the names of priests who stayed at Asuka-dera reveal that there were those from Koguryǒ as well as those from Paekche.

The Asuka-dera is distinctive not only in its plan, but also in the architectural features of the central enclosed buildings themselves. The podia of the pagoda and the central *kondō* are of ashlar masonry—square hewn stones arranged in rectangular series—that resemble what might be called the standard style used at Hōryū-ji and elsewhere, but the east and west *kondō* of Asuka-dera had two-stepped podia of rough uncoursed stone construction and small base stones arranged on top of the lower level (pl. 28). These relatively small base stones were probably used to support an outer row of pillars which held up the eaves. If such were the case, then these buildings were constructed in quite a different form from such extant buildings as the Hōryū-ji *kondō* and pagoda with their deeply extended eaves, generally considered one of the outstanding features of Buddhist architecture. In the Hōryū-ji structures, the deep eaves have been achieved by the support of cloud-shaped bracket complexes, eave purlins, tail rafters, and narrowed corner spans, eliminating the necessity for the additional row of eave supporting pillars. Of course, the exact method of construction at Asuka-dera can only be conjectured. The Asuka-dera type of two-stepped podia existed at temple sites in Paekche and Koguryŏ, and the Asuka-dera is clearly a case of imitation of Korean forms. But even in Korea this style was used only in the very early period of Buddhist architecture, and in Japan the form disappeared right after its use at Asuka-dera. Another Asuka-dera structure whose ancient foundation stones

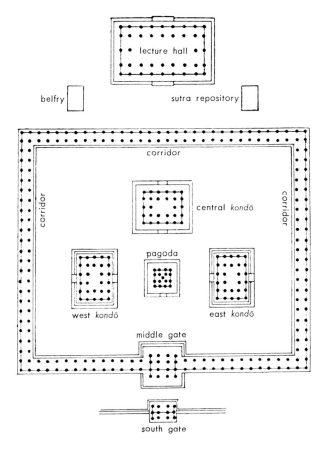

23. Restoration drawing of Asuka-dera plan.

remain is the middle gate, presumed to have been a three-bay by three-bay multi-storied building (pl. 29).

In the buildings erected prior to Hōryū-ji, as a general rule, the corner bays were square, and the hip rafters were placed on the diagonal, forming forty-five degree angles, but in the case of Asuka-dera, the measurements of the lengthwise and transverse bays were different, so that the corner bays were rectangular. Thus we must suppose that the roof support system of bracket complexes and the method of construction of these buildings, in general, were different from those used in later times. Here, again, we can see that Asuka-dera was made in a style distinct from those commonly known to us. Also excavated at the Asuka-dera are circular tiles that had been nailed to the cut ends of the roof rafters, and we can assume that the eaves of the central buildings were single and had circular rafters, and from the thickness of the rafters that the buildings were quite imposing.

45

24. Circular eave-end roof tile, Asuka-dera. (Nara National Research Institute of Cultural Properties)

26. Circular eave-end roof tile, Asuka-dera. (Nara National Research Institute of Cultural Properties)

25. Fragment of circular eave-end roof tile, Toyura-dera. (Tenri Sankōkan)

27. Circular eave-end roof tile, Asuka-dera. (Nara National Research Institute of Cultural Properties)

28. Remains of the two-stepped foundation of the east *kondō*, Asuka-dera. (Nara National Research Institute of Cultural Properties)

29. Remains of middle gate foundation, Asuka-dera. (Nara National Research Institute of Cultural Properties)

THE PAEKCHE STYLE

The Shitennō-ji in Osaka and the Wakakusa-dera (the original Hōryū-ji) in Nara were both built by Prince Shōtoku. There is some disagreement as to the date of the Shitennō-ji, but in view of the excavations at both the Shitennō-ji and at the Waka-kusa-dera of roof tiles made from the same mold, Shitennō-ji was most certainly built during the reign of Empress Suiko (r. 592–628), at about the same time as Wakakusa-dera. Both temples followed the arrangement popularly known as the Shitennō-ji plan, with the *kondō* placed behind the pagoda and on the same axis (pls. 30–31). Early Korean examples in this plan, which is also called the orthodox Paekche style, are numerous, and the Chūgū-ji, Yamada-dera, and, in fact, all temple remains of the Asuka period other than those of the Asuka-dera generally employ the same monastery plan. Since not only the plan but also the tiles of Shitennō-ji were in the Paekche mode, it is possible that this temple was a purer example of this style than the Asuka-dera.

The lecture hall (*kōdō*) of the Shitennō-ji seems to have been built in the mid-seventh

30. Aerial photograph of Shitennō-ji.

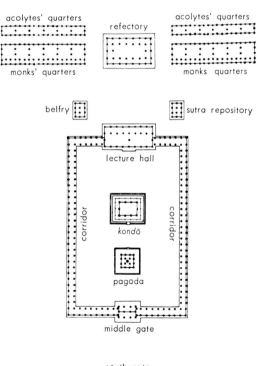

acolytes' quarters   refectory   acolytes' quarters

monks' quarters   monks quarters

belfry   sutra repository

lecture hall

corridor   kondō   corridor

pagoda

middle gate

31. Restoration drawing of Shitennō-ji plan.

south gate

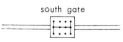

49

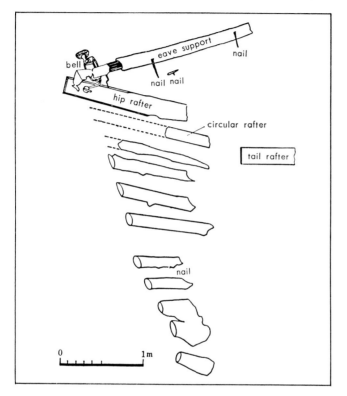

32. Traces of fan raftering excavated from the site of Shitennō-ji lecture hall.

century, slightly later than the *kondō* and pagoda. The corner eaves fell down during a typhoon, and while the wooden portions decayed, they left their imprint in the earth (pl. 32). The eaves were single and the circular rafters were arranged in a distinctive fanlike configuration, and the bracket complexes also had tail rafters passing through them. In China, from early times until the present, circular eave rafters arranged in fan shapes have been employed, but in Japan there are no other examples in Buddhist buildings until the importation of Sung building styles in the Kamakura period (1185–1330).

Once the imitation of Chinese architecture had begun, it was only natural that fan-shaped raftering would be introduced into Japan, and thus evidence of its use at Shitennō-ji is not surprising. One can assume that this arrangement was used at the Asuka-dera and Wakakusa-dera as well, but the question is why this formation disappeared in Japanese architecture with the building of the Hōryū-ji as it is known today. Taking fan raftering alone as a criterion of judgment, we can see that Asuka-period architecture possessed something distinct and separate from the Hōryū-ji style of architecture.

50

T'ANG-STYLE ARCHITECTURE

The Kawara-dera (Gubuku-ji) was built from 662 to 667, around the beginning of the Hakuhō period. The circular roof-tiles on eave ends used prior to this time, which were both of Paekche and Koguryŏ lineage, had a lotus flower design with single petals, but with the Kawara-dera the splendid T'ang-style roof tiles with double lotus-petal decoration came into use for the first time (pl. 34). The monastery plan also changed to a style with pagoda and west kondō balancing each other in the courtyard before the central kondō (pl. 35). The Kanzeon-ji of the government headquarters (dazai-fu) in Tsukushi, Kyushu, was constructed with roughly the same arrangement: pagoda and kondō placed opposite each other within a courtyard, and surrounded by a semienclosed roofed corridor. So too was the Sūfuku-ji in Ōmi province (now Shiga Prefecture), built at the wish of Emperor Tenji.

This style is followed in the west precinct of Hōryū-ji, the most celebrated example, and seen in many other contemporaneous sites such as the Koma-dera and the Sairin-ji. Since similar arrangements have not been found in China or Korea, some scholars believe that the temple plan originated in Japan. It has even been argued that, if the present Hōryū-ji has survived in its original form, Prince Shōtoku must have been the originator of this left-and-right plan, as that most congenial to the Japanese temperament. However, considering the fact that this temple plan suddenly became popular in the early Hakuhō period (662–710), it is more likely that its prototype was T'ang Chinese.

The Japanese temple closest to this prototype is probably the Kawara-dera, as indicated by the use there, for the first time in Japan, of T'ang double-petaled tiles on eave ends, as mentioned above. In addition, whereas the Asuka-dera and Shitennō-ji made use of the standard unit of measurement of the Korean Koguryŏ kingdom (the so-called koma-jaku, which equals approximately thirty-five centimeters), the Kawara-dera employs the shorter T'ang, or Tempyō, unit of thirty centimeters. In the central kondō of the Kawara-dera, the three central lengthwise bays are twelve T'ang shaku wide and both end bays ten shaku each. The Yakushi-ji and other buildings erected later are built on nearly the same scale. The Hōryū-ji kondō is divided into five bays lengthwise, but the three central bays measure nine koma-jaku each and the two end bays six shaku each, so that the ratio is 1:1.5, showing that the Hōryū-ji kondō had much narrower corner bays, relatively speaking, than the Kawara-dera central kondō. This ratio in the Hōryū-ji kondō is thought to result from the fact that, with the cloud-pattern bracket complex, the bracket arms and tail rafters supporting the eave purlins could be extended at only a 45° angle at the corners, and thus it was necessary to narrow the corner bays in order for the eave purlins to support safely the roof load above. Judging from this, it would seem that the Kawara-dera did not employ the same type of bracket system found at the Hōryū-ji. Moreover, instead of the single eaves with only base rafters used at Hōryū-ji, the eaves at Kawara-dera may have been doubled by the addition of flying rafters, another feature of T'ang origin.

33. Site of middle gate and west *kondō*, Kawara-dera. (Nara National Research Institute of Cultural Properties)

Eave rafters with two types of roof tile ends, for circular-ended base rafters and for square-ended flying rafters which compose double eaves, have also been found at the site of the Kita Yakushi-dō in Fukuoka Prefecture (*circa* 680). Thus double eaves, with the circular-ended base and square-ended flying eave rafters, are first seen in the Hakuhō period (662–710), and become the orthodox forms of Nara-period Buddhist halls.

The Hakuhō period is usually said to begin with the Taika coup d'etat of 645, but Buddhist architecture was a continuation of the Asuka style until about 661. After that, a new movement arose, one which was directly connected with T'ang style. The importation of T'ang-style architecture began with the Kawara-dera, and we may infer that a stylistic revolution in architecture occurred about this time.

34. Circular eave-end roof tile with double lotus petal design (above) and broad eave-end tile with incised lines (below), Kawara-dera. (Nara National Research Institute of Cultural Properties)

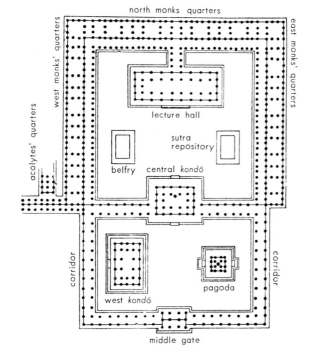

north monks quarters

west monks' quarters

east monks' quarters

acolytes' quarters

lecture hall

sutra repository

belfry

central *kondō*

corridor

west *kondō*

pagoda

corridor

middle gate

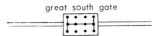

great south gate

35. Restoration drawing of Kawara-dera plan.

3

HŌRYŪ-JI

The Hōryū-ji monastery, located in the Ikaruga district in the countryside twenty kilometers south of Nara, is the most important surviving architectural complex of early Japan (pl. 37). No other site approaches it in historical importance or its fine state of preservation. No other site captures so well the atmosphere of an ancient monastery or holds so rich an array of paintings, sculptures, and ritual implements.

The nucleus of the Hōryū-ji west precinct (pl. 36) is composed of the buildings which were the standard for the Japanese monastic compound throughout the ancient period: the *kondō*, or main hall, wherein is enshrined the main devotional image of the monastery; the pagoda, which can be presumed to have developed in part from the Indian stupa, to enshrine a holy relic and thereby symbolize the presence of a Buddhist sanctuary; the semienclosed roofed corridor, surrounding the holiest sector of the monastery; the middle gate, which gives access to that sector; the great south gate, on the same axis as the middle gate, but much farther in front, and serving as the main entrance to the entire monastery compound; the lecture hall, a building large enough to seat the monks while they assemble for instructions and prayers; the belfry, wherein is suspended the bell which signals the events of the monastic day from beginning to end; the sutra repository, which stores holy texts; the dormitories, which house the tiny cells where the monks sleep and store their meager possessions; and finally the refectory, bath house, and other utilitarian structures for abbots, monks, and their helpers.

MONASTERY PLAN

The four structures of the Hōryū-ji west precinct which are recognized as late seventh century in date are the *kondō* (pls. 39, 41–42), pagoda (pl. 38), middle gate (pls. 40, 45), and semienclosed roofed corridor (pl. 43). The *kondō* and pagoda are laid out opposite each other, east and west, and the middle gate is located between and in front of them, at the center front of the roofed corridor (pl. 36). Looking to the right and left from the two-story middle gate, one sees the massive *kondō* and the light, taller pagoda; the relationship between them is a harmonious balance between tall and low units.

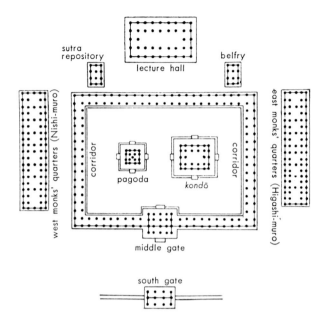

sutra repository

lecture hall

belfry

west monks' quarters (Nishi-muro)

east monks' quarters (Higashi-muro)

corridor

pagoda

kondō

corridor

middle gate

south gate

36. Restoration drawing of plan of Hōryū-ji west precinct.

The semienclosed roofed corridor is today attached to the sutra repository and belfry and, turning sharply, is also connected with the lecture hall. Originally, however, the roofed corridor surrounded only *kondō* and pagoda. This monastery plan, an abbreviated version of that at the Kawara-dera, is suited to small temples. There are many examples of it in regional clan temples like the Koma-dera in Kyoto Prefecture, Miroku-ji in Gifu Prefecture, Sairin-ji in Osaka, Ina-dera in Hyōgo Prefecture, and the remains of the Itami-dera, also in Hyōgo Prefecture.

At the time of its founding at the command of Prince Shōtoku, Hōryū-ji (then called Wakakusa-dera) was a large temple compound. However, with the destruction of the family of Prince Shōtoku's son, Prince Yamashiro no Ōe, by Soga no Iruka in 643, which effectively ended Prince Shōtoku's line, Hōryū-ji (that is, Wakakusa-dera) lost its original patrons, and, at the time of its rebuilding after destruction by fire, had become little more than a regional monastery. It was probably for this reason that the original Shitennō-ji plan (suitable for large temples) was abandoned in the rebuilding and the small-temple arrangement adopted in its place. In contrast to the strict bilateral symmetry of the older scheme, with hall and pagoda in a straight line (pl. 31), there was now a more informal, even asymmetrical plan. No matter what the specific reason for the employment of this plan at Hōryū-ji, there is no doubt that this arrangement appealed to the Japanese temperament by virtue of its soft asymmetry of massive *kondō* and towering pagoda. That this plan enjoyed considerable popularity before the introduction of T'ang architecture indicates that the early Hakuhō period (662–710) was one of transition from Paekche and Koguryŏ models to those of the T'ang dynasty.

55

37. Aerial view of west precinct, Hōryū-ji.
Seen clearly from the air is the west precinct of Hōryū-ji as it stands today, the site which best preserves the basic components of the early Japanese Buddhist monastery. Just northeast of of the parking lot in the bottom left of the photograph is the great south gate, through which pilgrim and tourist alike enter on foot. Connected to the great south gate by a path, which is part of the main north-south axis of the monastery, is the middle gate, adjoined by the semienclosed roofed corridor on its east and west. This corridor surrounds the nucleus of the monastery. Enclosed within are the two most important symbolic structures, the five-story pagoda and the *kondō*. One unusual feature of this plan is the dimensions of the corridor, eleven bays from the middle gate to the east side of the monastery and only ten bays from the middle gate to the west, accommodating the larger dimensions of the *kondō* and the smaller pagoda on its respective

sides. On the same axis as the great south gate and middle gate are the main lecture hall (Daikōdō) and a building of a later period. The small, roofed structures southeast and southwest of the lecture hall are the belfry and sutra repository, both also adjoining the corridor. East and west beyond this corridor are the Higashi-muro and Nishi-muro. Just east of the Higashi-muro is the Tsuma-muro. These three buildings served as living quarters for priests and novices. The east-west oriented building just east and slightly to the north of them is the refectory and *hosodono* (a shallow, detached forehall), and the Kōfū-zō storehouse is to their south, east of the Tsuma-muro. Three newer storage halls and the museum in which are housed many of the Hōryū-ji treasures are to the far right of the photograph, and beyond them, outside of the picture, is the east precinct, famous for the Yumedono and the Dempō-dō.

DISTINCTIVE ARCHITECTURAL DETAILS

The Hōryū-ji *kondō*, pagoda, and middle gate are of nearly the same style, all employing a roof support system consisting of the cloud-shaped brackets discussed above and
single eaves with square rafters. Because of recent skillful repairs, the *kondō* and
pagoda have been restored to nearly the same appearance as at the time of their
building. In the middle gate, however, may be seen penetrating tie-beams added
by later generations, and the roof is in the form given it by an Edo-period reconstruction; these later remodeled portions make the structure somewhat ponderous in
appearance.

Characteristic of the Hōryū-ji style are the massive circular columns which are
given distinct entasis—swelling of the central part of the shaft, a method used by the
Greeks to correct the optical illusion of concavity which would result if the columns
were perfectly straight (pl. 45). Atop each column is a plate (*saraita*) to which is
joined a large bearing block and the rest of the bracket complex. Among the brackets
are cloud-shaped forms (pls. 45–46) engraved with spirals that, at first glance, suggest
the shapes of birds or beasts; the lower slightly protruding portion of these brackets
are called *zetsu* ("tongues") and create a sculpturesque effect. In fact, throughout
the Hōryū-ji structure may be found strongly plastic, curvilinear elements. On the
exterior, the second-story balustrades (pl. 47) are supported by curved inverted V-
shaped struts, alternating with three-block brackets—three small bearing blocks
supported by a bracket arm, carried on a principal bearing block. Together with the
fretwork pattern, the wood joinery of the balustrade follows a decorative design
rather than an architectonic mode of construction.

38.   Five-story pagoda, Hōryū-ji.

Such details exist in stone structures in China and Korea. At the rock-cut temples of Yün-kang, T'ien-lung shan, and Mai-chi shan, especially, are many analogous elements dating from roughly the mid-sixth century. Yet, among them there is no suitable example of the cloud-shaped bracket, the distinctive characteristic of the temples in the Ikaruga area—Hōryū-ji, Hokki-ji, and Hōrin-ji (pagoda now rebuilt) —as well as the miniature Tamamushi Shrine at Hōryū-ji. These are the only extant examples. About all we can say is that the cloud-shaped bracket might be in the tradition of the curved bracket arms seen in second-century stone gate pillars of the Later Han dynasty; since the cloud-shaped bracket does not occur in the Chinese rock-cut cave temples of the fifth century onward, it is thought that it might derive from the older architectural style.

On the whole, it seems that this combination of ancient stylistic elements and new details which we see at Hōryū-ji did not take place in China; perhaps no buildings just like the *kondō* or pagoda of Hōryū-ji were built there. In Korea, on the other hand, which became a repository of Chinese influences, it is presumed that new and old were mixed together, and it is there that the same kind of complexities characteristic of Asuka architecture can be seen.

Because the methods of joinery were undeveloped, the distinguishing characteristic of the structural surface is a system of simply piling members upward; the pillars, to prevent horizontal sway, were made unnecessarily heavy (thick in diameter) in relation to the load above, and on each side of the structure long bracket tie-beams were placed one above the other, meeting at the corners in a dovetail fashion.

59

39. *Kondō*, Hōryū-ji.

The *kondō*, erected, at latest, sometime after 670, is thought to be the oldest of the Hōryū-ji structures. Resting on a masonry foundation built in two levels, it is a relatively small structure measuring only five bays in length and four in depth. Attached to the ground floor is a *mokoshi* with a wooden plank roof, enclosing the building on four sides. The roofs of the first and second stories are covered with heavy grey tiles. The upper story, though considerably smaller than the first, is nonetheless in harmony with it. The hip-and-gable roof of the upper story, with its sharply sloping contours, adds to the sense of strength and solemnity. The cloud-pattern brackets of the *kondō* have incised curvilinear lines along their edges, and the entasis of the pillars is the strongest too. These and other features give the *kondō* an overall feeling of the archaic stone architecture of China, which had been transmitted through Korea to Japan in the Asuka period.

40. Middle gate, Hōryū-ji.

It was common for the middle gate to have an odd number of bays with the central one serving as the entrance and the two end bays housing images of guardian figures. The Hōryū-ji middle gate is unusual in that it is four bays across with a two-bay entrance. Thus, in the very center are pillars, where the main entrance is in the usual three-bay-wide gate. The two-storied gate is three bays deep, in contrast to the usual two bays, apparently in order to balance its unusual width. The serious consideration given to size and external harmony is characteristic of early Buddhist architecture.

61

41. *Kondō*, Hōryū-ji.

42. *Kondō* interior, Hōryū-ji.

43. Corridor, Hōryū-ji.

The semienclosed roofed corridor surrounds the
monastery nucleus, connects one building of a
monastery to another, or encloses one or more
buildings within a precinct. The Hōryū-ji roofed
corridor serves a dual function—an enclosure
for the *kondō* and five-story pagoda and a connecting passageway between the middle gate,
belfry, lecture hall, and sutra repository. It is
the oldest surviving such corridor in Japan.
Special features of the pillars of the roofed corridors in the Hakuhō and early Tempyō periods
are the entasis and the placement of the pillars
atop foundation stones, also found at the Asuka-
dera, but not at the Kōfuku-ji of the later
Heijō capital. Although the rainbow beams and
diagonal struts are somewhat thin, they stand in
good relation to the large pillars. The entire
rainbow beam is curved in a charmingly
unsophisticated way, a style which is older and
simpler than that of the Tempyō era, when such
beams curved only at each end.

65

44. Middle gate bracket system, Hōryū-ji.

45. Middle gate, Hōryū-ji.

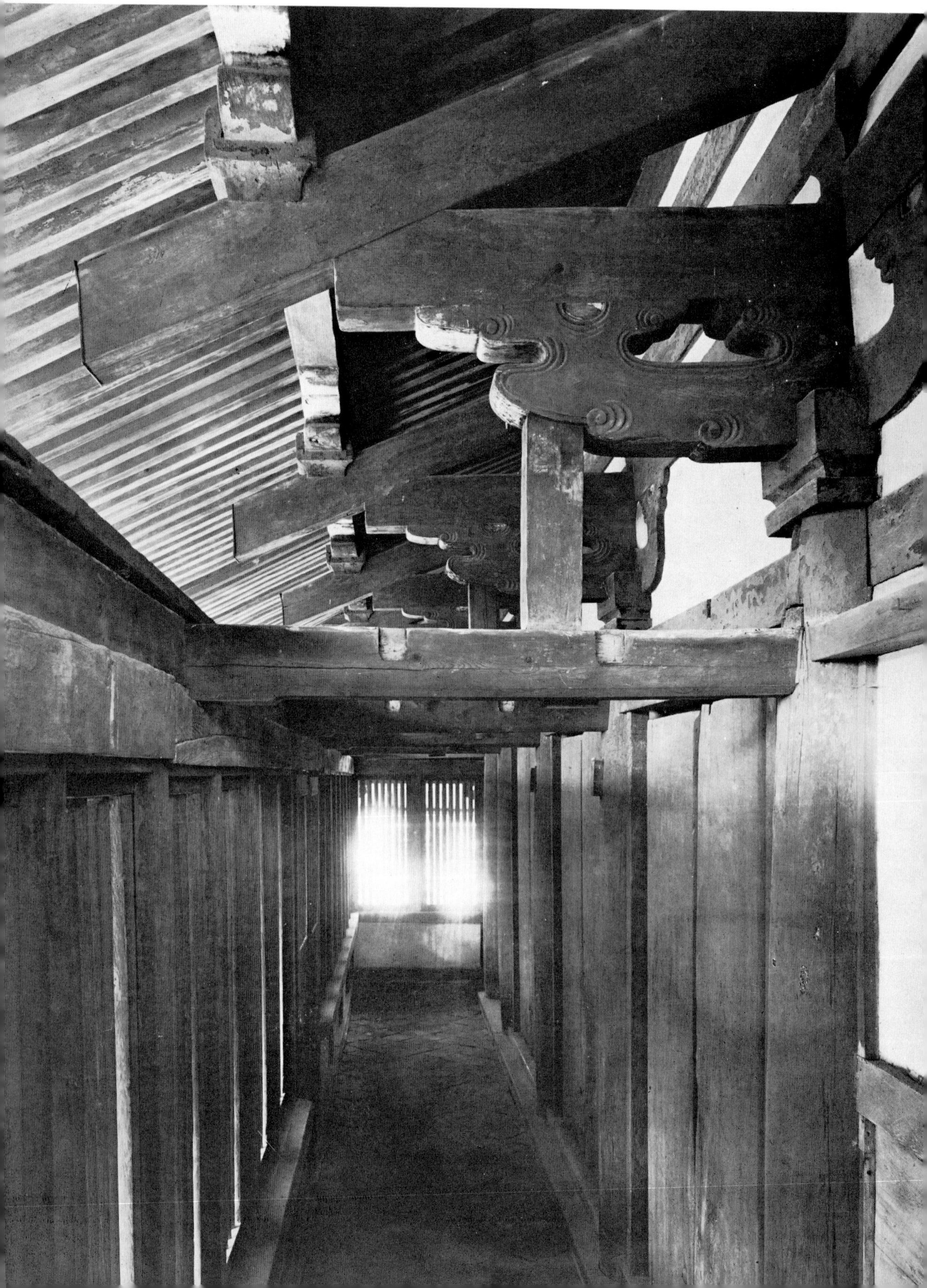

47. *Kondō* upper story, Hōryū-ji.

46. Bracket system of *kondō* first story, Hōryū-ji.

48. Eaves on first story of five-story pagoda, Hōryū-ji.

The square, parallel rafters supporting the eaves can be considered completely Japanese in style (pl. 48). Circular rafters were common in China, perhaps because good timber was difficult to obtain there (it is somewhat wasteful to square-off round logs). Reflecting Chinese custom, the Asuka-dera and Shitennō-ji both had round rafters (pl. 49). In general, however, Japanese architecture used cut timbers because it is easier to build with square rafters. For this reason, all rafters in ancient Shinto shrines were square.

Arranging the roof rafters in a fan shape to distribute the roof load as equally as possible is a logical arrangement and even today the thatched roofs of Japanese farmhouses are often constructed in this manner. However, when one looks at the undersides of the deeply projecting eaves, they lack a feeling of strict order and stability. On the other hand, in the parallel rafter arrangment, although the entire weight of all the rafters from the purlin outward falls on the hip rafter, the resulting effect is extremely orderly (pl. 48). Because the Japanese were long familiar with shrine architecture and its gabled-roof construction and parallel rafters, they abandoned the Chinese circular rafters in a fan-shaped arrangement and replaced them in Buddhist temple architecture with square rafters in a parallel arrangement. Just when the shift occurred is uncertain, but it was probably one aspect of the cultural changes at the beginning of the Hakuhō period. There is a certain amount of disharmony between the form of the wide overhang made of straight timbers and the curvilinear design of the piled-up bracket complexes and the framework, and in this we sense their origins in a era of transition.

49. *Kondō* eaves with fan raftering (reconstruction), Shitennō-ji.

Structural Balance

The proportions of the parts of the Hōryū-ji *kondō* and pagoda achieve an exquisite balance. In both, the upper stories are successively diminished in scale; in the pagoda the fifth-story framework is just one-half that of the first story—a far greater diminution than would be seen in later buildings, imparting a lightness combined with stability as it towers upward (pl. 38). Interestingly, the spans between the pillars of the *kondō* and pagoda are of decidedly simple proportions, as we shall see below, giving rise to a beauty of exterior form that is by no means accidental.

In establishing the proportions of the pagoda the master builders employed a module which measured .75 of the Korean Koguryŏ *shaku* (*koma-jaku*; approximately thirty-five centimeters). The central bay of the bottom story measures ten units wide; the two flanking bays are each seven units—a total of twenty-four units wide, or eighteen *koma-jaku* (approximately 6.4 meters). For the upper portions the total width of the framework of each story decreases by three modular units. On the second story the central bay measures nine units, the flanking bays are six each; on the third story they are eight and five, respectively; on the fourth they are seven and four; the fifth story is but two bays wide, each bay being six units. The surface area of each story decreases as one goes up, but the sizes of the support system and timbers change little, and the wooden members become more crowded. It is because of this crowding that the fifth story is divided into only two bays, and the resolution of the details lapses into imbalance. Nonetheless, the entire form is quite well-ordered. The serious consideration given to the overall balance of the structure is a characteristic that will be shared with the architecture of the Tempyō period in the eighth century—and indeed is the secret of much of the beauty of early Buddhist buildings.

71

50. Foundation stone of Wakakusa-dera pagoda, Hōryū-ji. (Nara National Research Institute of Cultural Properties)

51. Roof tiles excavated from Wakakusa-dera site, Hōryū-ji. (Hōryū-ji)

52. Roof tiles excavated from Hōryū-ji west precinct. (Hōryū-ji)

DATE OF CONSTRUCTION

There have been long-standing disputes over the date of the Hōryū-ji buildings. One theory has held that the Hōryū-ji buildings remain unchanged from the time of their construction by Prince Shōtoku in the reign of Empress Suiko (592–628). Opposing this is a view based on the entry in the *Nihon shoki* which records that, on the thirtieth day of the fourth month of 670, "a fire broke out. Not a single building was left." This second theory then assumes that all buildings on the site were reconstructed after 670. Excavations have revealed a temple site, the Wakakusa-dera, just southeast of where the Hōryū-ji stands today (pl. 50). It is recorded as having been built to the west of the Ikaruga Palace of Prince Shōtoku, and, as was common in the Asuka period, the two were adjoined as a temple-palace unit. The Wakakusa-dera excavations have revealed a square-shaped pagoda 13.5 meters on each side, a *kondō* of 22 by 19.5 meters, arranged on the same axis, about twenty degrees out of line from the polar star, suggesting that the temple was worked into the available space after the building of Ikaruga Palace. The layout was the same as that of the Shitennō-ji (pl. 31), which was also commissioned by Prince Shōtoku. The present Hōryū-ji buildings are on a strict north-south axis, and their arrangement shows a departure from the Shitennō-ji plan of pagoda and *kondō* on the same axis. It is assumed that the Wakakusa-dera burned to the ground in 670, and that the post-670 Hōryū-ji was moved slightly to the north and built anew, making possible the accurate alignment with the North Star.

In any case, the construction of the present *kondō* was completed by the first years of the reign of Emperor Temmu (673–686). Next was the pagoda; the middle gate and roofed semienclosed corridor were built in the last years of the seventh century.

The construction date places the Hōryū-ji after the Kawara-dera and at about the same time as the Yakushi-ji, which will be described below.

There are many essential differences between the Hōryū-ji and the two temples assumed by scholars to be in the T'ang style—the Kawara-dera and the Yakushi-ji. On the roof tiles, for example, we find a similar double lotus-petal pattern at Hōryū-ji and at Kawara-dera, but we recognize a slight difference in the lines that divide each petal and the whorl leaves within the petals, which suggests a different lineage (pls. 34, 52). Judging from the older style of structural elements such as the cloud-shaped brackets, there is no reason to doubt that the Hōryū-ji has a place within the Asuka style, in fact that it is one branch of that variegated style. But there are also distinct Japanese improvements, and thus the Hōryū-ji style is seen to be a product of the early Hakuhō transitional period.

HIGASHI-MURO

The Higashi-muro (Eastern Residence; pls. 53–54) is the Hōryū-ji building next in age after the *kondō*, pagoda, middle gate, and semienclosed roofed corridor. It was built as a dwelling for monks, probably at the end of the seventh century, after the completion of the outer enclosure of the Hōryū-ji nucleus. Built in a simple, practical manner, its pillars are connected directly to the beams without bracketing, in a manner structurally similar to that of shrine architecture. It is extremely interesting that such a building should be constructed so differently from the contemporaneous neighboring structures with their cloud-shaped bracket systems. Nonetheless, the feeling for construction is not the same as that of some shrine architecture which has chiefly straight members. The pillars have entasis, and overhead in the interior are the finely curved rainbow beams (*kōryō*) similar to those found in the roofed corridor. Circular rafters are used, and are thought to be old timbers used originally when Hōryū-ji (Wakakusa-dera) was first established and then, after some repair, reused; some old materials were also converted to use for pillars and pillar base stones. The Higashi-muro therefore seems to transmit the tradition of Asuka architecture.

Higashi-muro underwent major repairs repeatedly during its later history. The present structure has been restored to the appearance of its 1365 rebuilding, but at the northern end the interiors of the two chambers for monks have been restored to their original appearance. Higashi-muro is an important structure in which one can see the actual conditions of an ancient monk's dormitory (pl. 55).

HŌRIN-JI AND HOKKI-JI

Buildings which are architecturally similar to those of the Hōryū-ji are the three-story pagoda of the Hokki-ji and the three-story pagoda of the Hōrin-ji, the latter destroyed in 1944 in a fire caused by lightning. Both of these small monasteries are located a short distance northeast of Hōryū-ji, and like the Hōryū-ji, their histories in some accounts are tied in with the life of Prince Shōtoku and his family. The Hōrin-ji plan is identical to that of Hōryū-ji, but on a much smaller scale. The plan of Hokki-ji has both pagoda and *kondō* surrounded by a semienclosed roofed corridor, but their positions are the reverse of the Hōryū-ji and the Hōrin-ji. The three-story pagoda at Hokki-ji (pl. 56) was built in 706, and documents the survival of the style to that date. At this time, the popularity of the early T'ang mode as represented by Dai-kandai-ji and Yakushi-ji had gained momentum, and the style of Hōrin-ji and Hokki-ji had become a conservative preserve of the Ikaruga area, in which Hōryū-ji is located.

53. Higashi-muro, Hōryū-ji.

54. Higashi-muro, Hōryū-ji.

56. Three-story pagoda, Hokki-ji.

55. Higashi-muro interior (restored),
Hōryū-ji.

77

4

FROM THE FUJIWARA
TO THE HEIJŌ CAPITAL

ADOPTION OF THE T'ANG SYSTEM

Buddhist architecture was prospering by the end of the seventh century through the enthusiastic patronage of Emperor Temmu (r. 673–686) and Empress Jitō (r. 686–697) and their courts, and qualitative changes in the character of building are apparent. The official exchange of envoys with T'ang China—no longer by way of Korea—facilitated Japan's direct absorption of Chinese culture. After the Taika Reforms of 646, the Japanese made a strong and continuous effort to change to governmental institutions and modes of operation modeled on those of T'ang China. Along with the gradual completion of the legal system, we see in the last decade of the seventh century the beginnings of a new, epoch-making movement in architecture: it is the construction of Fujiwara-kyō, Japan's first effort to create a permanent capital city.

Until the mid-seventh century the capital changed locations with each new emperor, and, consisting mostly of the imperial palace, was built on a small scale. The 646 imperial edict enacting the Taika Reforms changed the land system from one of clan management to one of government control, and along with the enforcement of government distribution of land there was a provision to create a Chinese-style capital city. In 652 the Nagara Toyosaki Palace, recorded to have been in the T'ang palatial style, was erected, and for the first time all government officials were housed within the imperial grounds, a custom that was to continue. The palace built in the reign of Emperor Tenji (661–671) at Ōtsu in Shiga Prefecture (ancient Ōmi province) and the Kiyomihara Palace built in Asuka during the time of Emperor Temmu (673–686) progressed to the point of giving the official titles of right and left sectors to the capital city, but nevertheless there are many unanswered questions regarding the extent to which these palaces had actually become the centers of fully developed cities.

The effort to perfect a centralized political authority and national unity based on T'ang Chinese systems soon resulted in the *jōbō* system for the uniform division of land in the capital and the *jōri* system in the countryside, both based upon a grid system of standard units. The Fujiwara capital, begun in 691, the year following the

57. Earthen foundation at southeast section of main palace, Fujiwara palace site. (Nara National Research Institute of Cultural Properties)

belated coronation of Empress Jitō, and occupied by 694, was the first Japanese city built with this grid system of streets running north-south and east-west. Its layout imitated that of the T'ang-dynasty capitals of Ch'ang-an and Lo-yang. The palace was raised near the center of the city at the north end, and left and right to the south were the two great temples Daikandai-ji and Yakushi-ji.

The Building of Daikandai-ji and Yakushi-ji

In the Temmu era (673–686) the nationalization of Buddhism was stronger than ever before, and a system of officially sponsored state temples was established. Daikandai-ji and Yakushi-ji were built by the temple construction bureau, which was a government building organization especially set up for this purpose. Just as at Ch'ang-an and Lo-yang, temples were, along with palaces, among the most important elements in city planning. The Daikandai-ji and Yakushi-ji were built on a grander scale than had been seen in past temples, in order to increase the capital's symbolic significance as the seat of authority of a centralized government. Adding the Asuka-dera and the Kawara-dera to these two temples inside the capital, there were now four great temples, and they became the centers of the devotions and grand vegetarian feasts of the imperial court. It was natural that the upsurge of Buddhism, along with the   79

58. Pagoda site, Daikandai-ji.

59. Roof tiles from Daikandai-ji: above, circular eave-end tile (Nara Prefectural Archaeology Museum); below, broad eave-end tile (Nara National Research Institute of Cultural Properties).

importance of the temples in city planning and the organization of a government bureau for building temples, would speed up the adoption of the T'ang architectural style.

The Daikandai-ji (pl. 58) was successor to the Kudaradai-ji, construction of which had begun in 639. When the Kudaradai-ji was damaged by fire, it was renamed and moved to a new location north of the Kiyomihara Palace, where it was reconstructed. This second location was later included within the confines of the Fujiwara capital, and the temple completed during the reign of Emperor Mommu (697–707). Its remains bear a resemblance to the Kawara-dera monastery plan, but its scale was larger in every respect. In plan the pagoda measured 16.3 meters on each side of the first story and was nine stories high, displaying a grandeur hitherto unseen. The roof tiles of this temple have the same double lotus pattern as has been found at the Kawara-dera, but in addition there is a bead pattern around the petals that was directly imported from T'ang China (pl. 59). Roof tiles decorated with this bead motif were also used in the Fujiwara Palace, and remained part of the main current of official architecture of the Nara and Heian periods. Judging from the roof tile remains, one would think that a more advanced T'ang style than the one seen at the Kawara-dera is found here, but unfortunately excavations are not complete.

60. Stone bases for pillars of the *kondō*, Moto
Yakushi-ji (Fujiwara capital).

The temple at which the importation of the early T'ang style is clearly evident, from
the foundation remains alone, is the Yakushi-ji. In 680 Emperor Temmu made an
imperial vow to build the temple, but the actual building began sometime after 687,
during the rule of Empress Jitō. Its construction went forward with the building of
the Fujiwara capital, and was completed around 698. In this monastery arrangement, the *kondō* is situated inside the semienclosed roofed corridor, and to the left
and right in front of it are two pagodas, facing each other. The general rule of the
single pagoda is now broken.

The same ground plan is found in Korea, which had been unified in 676 under
the rule of the Silla kings. There, early T'ang civilization was absorbed and a high
Buddhist culture created. Beginning with the Sa'ch'on-wang sa (Shitennō-ji in Japanese) of 679, the United Silla Capital of Kyŏngju saw the building of many monasteries with paired pagodas. There is thus no question that the early T'ang style began
to flourish in Silla and in Japan at about the same time.

The Yakushi-ji of the Fujiwara capital is now called the Moto-Yakushi-ji (Original Yakushi-ji) to distinguish it from the temple after it was transferred to the Heijō
capital. Today only foundation stones of the original Yakushi-ji remain (pl. 60), but
in the move to the new capital, buildings of the same scale and arrangement as the

81

original were constructed. The present east pagoda, the only one of these buildings to have come down to us, seems thus to have continued the architectural style of its original form in the Fujiwara capital (pl. 1).

THE TRANSFER OF THE CAPITAL TO HEIJŌ

In 701, the first year of Taihō, on New Year's morning, a great ceremony had been held to celebrate pride in the Fujiwara capital, which was thought to have reached the level of T'ang culture. It was felt that "the matter of culture and institutions had been completed" with the accomplishment of this capital. But only seven years later, in 708, Empress Gemmei issued a proclamation ordering the transfer of the capital to Heijō. The Fujiwara capital, occupying a narrow site surrounded by the three Yamato mountains, proved just large enough to contain the imperial palaces and related official residences, but could not accommodate a general urban area. Because of the new Taihō Civil Code, the capital city's population rapidly increased as the authority of the central government strengthened, and the need arose for a much larger imperial capital. Thus, in the year 710, the capital was moved to Heijō, near the site of the modern Nara, and great temples of the Asuka region and the Fujiwara capital were transferred one after the other to the new capital site. Architectural projects were undertaken to an unprecedented degree.

The Heijō capital was a city modeled after the plan of the T'ang capital of Ch'ang-an. The wide blocks of its checkered arrangement (pl. 61) spanned about 4.3 kilometers east to west and 4.9 kilometers north to south. The capital was divided into left and right sectors, each nine blocks north to south by four blocks east to west. Each block was further divided into sixteen plots of land. East of the left sector of the capital was the "outer sector," an area of 2.2 kilometers north to south by 1.6 kilometers east to west. The Heijō capital was the second largest city in East Asia at that time (the largest was Ch'ang-an), and its estimated population during its most flourishing period was 200,000 people. Comparing Heijō to Ch'ang-an, which was 9.6 kilometers east to west and 8.2 kilometers north to south, the Japanese capital was only one-third the size of the Chinese city.

At the center of the north end of the Heijō capital was the imperial palace, occupying an estimated area of 960 meters by 960 meters. Recently it has become clear that an eastern precinct (tō-in) was later added, measuring about 240 meters east to west and 720 north to south. Within the palace compound, imposing mainland-style buildings like the Chōdō-in with tile roofs did exist, but were confined to the central area and served administrative purposes. The area containing the residence of the emperor and those of the court officials contained buildings of generally simpler construction, with roofs in the native style covered with cypress bark or planks and supported by pillars implanted in the earth without foundation stones (pl. 62).

In contrast, Buddhist pagodas five and seven stories high soared overhead. Seen

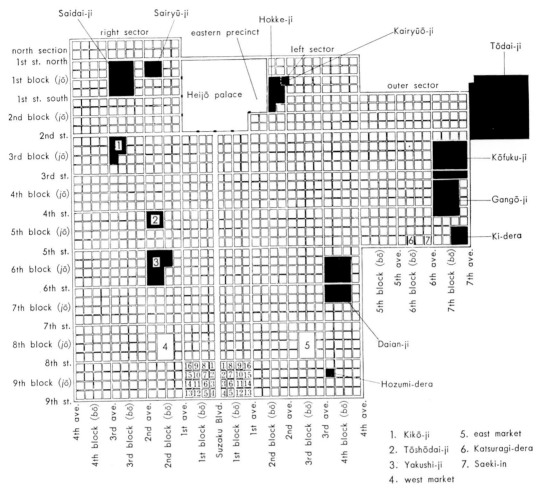

61. Restoration drawing of Heijō capital plan (viewed from east to west, the rows of large blocks of land are called *jō*, from north to south *bō*; each block is divided into sixteen smaller plots (*machi* or *chō*) and numbered, two examples of which are given at bottom of map).

from afar they signaled the presence of the monasteries, where first the *kondō* with their gleaming golden *shibi* (tail-shaped tiles at the ends of the roof ridges; see pl. 94 for examples) and then other temple halls with plastered white walls, pillars painted in Chinese red and vertically latticed windows painted green, decked the capital city in an aura of grandeur. In contrast to the low residences with board roofs, these conspicuously prominent symbols of an advanced civilization recall the ancient poem from the eighth-century *Man'yōshū*:*

* *The Manyōshū: The Nippon Gakujutsu Shinkōkai Translation of One Thousand Poems.* (1940; reprinted, New York and London: Columbia University Press, 1969), p. 97.

83

62. Excavation of principal hall of emperor's quarters at Heijō palace site.

The Imperial City of fairest Nara
  Glows now at the height of beauty,
Like brilliant flowers in bloom!

Buddhist structures in the brilliant T'ang-period style were intentionally erected from the very onset of the building of the Heijō capital as symbols of advanced civilization. In 710, the man who led the movement to transfer the capital, Fujiwara no Fuhito, shifted at the same time his own clan temple, Yamashina-dera (also called Umayasaka-dera), from an unidentified site to one in the outer sector, third street, seventh avenue, where it occupied an area of sixteen plots of land (16 *chō*, or 480 meters by 480 meters). It was renamed Kōfuku-ji (pl. 61). Next, official temples of the Asuka and Fujiwara sites were also transferred one by one. In 716 the Daikandai-ji was moved to the block at sixth street, third avenue, in the left sector of the capital and renamed Daian-ji; in 718 the Gangō-ji (formerly the Asuka-dera) was moved to the block at third and fourth streets, sixth avenue, of the outer sector, south of Kōfuku-ji; and at the same time the original Yakushi-ji, retaining the name Yakushi-ji, was transferred and rebuilt on the block at the fifth street, second avenue, in the right sector of the capital, so that the Daian-ji and the Yakushi-ji occupied roughly corresponding sites in the left and right sectors.

63. Kikō-ji and grounds.

The reason that Kawara-dera (Gufuku-ji) did not take part in the move to Heijō, but gave place to Kōfuku-ji, is uncertain, but in any case the four great temples connected with the Fujiwara capital—Daikandai-ji, the original Yakushi-ji, Asuka-dera, and Kawara-dera—were replaced by Daian-ji, Yakushi-ji, Gangō-ji, and Kō-fuku-ji, respectively, as the four great temples of the Heijō capital. There are still many unclear points concerning the actual state of affairs of this transfer, but we believe that, in general, the buildings of the monastery nuclei remained on their original Fujiwara sites, and temple buildings of the new capital were built completely anew. Even the removal of secondary equipment like images and minor buildings seems to have been limited in scope.

In 722, the Haji clan commenced the building of Kikō-ji (Sugawara-dera; pl. 63) in the block at the second street, third avenue, of the right sector of the capital. Privately patronized temples of a similar sort were built within all areas of the capital—the Ki-dera by the Ki clan, the Katsuragi-dera by the Katsuragi clan, and the Saeki-in by the Saeki clan, so that like Ch'ang-an and Lo-yang, Heijō came to be a colorful city filled with a great number of Buddhist temples.

An entry for 724 in the *Shoku Nihongi* (History of Japan Continued) expresses the power of the body politic: "The capital is where the people of the many regions come

85

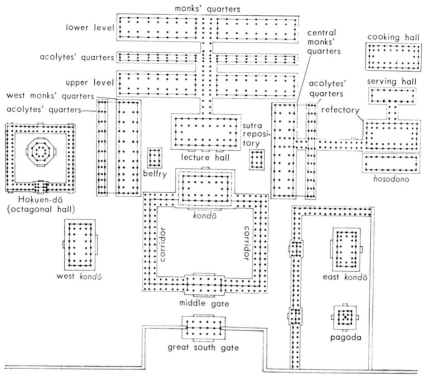

64. Restoration drawing of Kōfuku-ji plan.

to court; were it not splendid, how could it display its virtue?" Politically propelled, the role of temple architecture at the Heijō capital must be seen as one much more strongly colored by government influence than was the case at the Fujiwara capital.

ARCHITECTURAL FEATURES OF THE FOUR GREAT TEMPLES

The four great temples were built in approximately the thirty-year period between 710 and 740, so that there was a general similarity in architectural construction. However, the plan of each had its own specific character. We know that there were differences in the architectural styles of these Nara pagodas and halls from the records of the Heian aristocrats who later came to worship in them.

The principle hitherto observed of *kondō* and pagoda, that they be placed inside the same semienclosed roofed corridor, was broken at the Kōfuku-ji (pl. 64). Entering via the great south gate and middle gate, there was only the *kondō* at the center, facing the enclosed courtyard; the pagoda was moved into a separate precinct to the east. Such an epoch-making change was probably made in imitation of a style of the flourishing T'ang dynasty. From the Tempyō period (711–781) on, the arrangement of pagoda and *kondō* in separate precincts became the most popular.

65.   Restoration model of Daian-ji. (See also plate 165.)

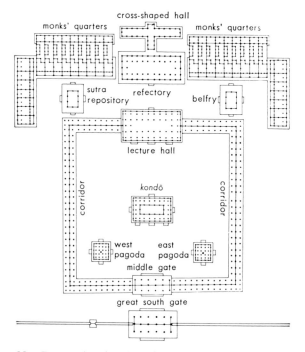

monks' quarters cross-shaped hall monks' quarters

sutra repository refectory belfry

lecture hall

corridor kondō corridor

west pagoda east pagoda

middle gate

great south gate

66. Restoration drawing of Yakushi-ji plan.

The Daian-ji was built with the twin east and west pagoda precincts in front and outside of the great south gate (pls. 65, 165). Begun in 718 under the guidance of the monk Dōji, who had returned from China in the same year, it can be assumed that it reflected the latest technology from T'ang China. The Yakushi-ji, on the other hand, was a revival of the form as it was at the Fujiwara capital (pl. 66). The Gangō-ji had the pagoda set apart (pl. 172), as did the Kōfuku-ji (pl. 64), but its *kondō* remained standing independently inside the area surrounded by the semienclosed roofed corridor, preserving the system used in Asuka and Hakuhō times; it was thus outside the tradition of the Tempyō-period system from Kōfuku-ji onward, in which the *kondō* was penetrated on both sides by the roofed corridor.

It is probable that the arrangement and the architectural style of each monastery were somewhat different because there were different T'ang-dynasty architectural models. Each of the four great temples competitively sought its own unique characteristics, and zealously imitated T'ang styles. The rate at which Chinese forms were absorbed during this period is astonishing.

$\frac{5}{}$

YAKUSHI-JI AND THE ARCHITECTURE
OF THE EARLY TEMPYŌ PERIOD

Yakushi-ji—Conforming to the Older Style

The Yakushi-ji of the Fujiwara capital was completed by the year 698, but soon after this, the capital was moved to Heijō. About the year 718 the construction of the new temple was begun. The east pagoda is the only structure remaining from the Yakushi-ji as it was rebuilt in the Heijō capital, and we presume from later records that it was erected by the year 730. Some scholars think that the buildings themselves were transferred, for not only are the roof tiles used at the new Yakushi-ji exactly the same as those used at the older temple in the Fujiwara capital, but the base stones of the new Yakushi-ji are completely identical in scale to those of the east and west pagodas of the original Yakushi-ji. However, records of the Tempyō period indicate that there were four Yakushi-ji pagodas, stating that two were still standing at the original site. Therefore, the two at the Heijō capital would seem to be not transfers, but newly built pagodas.

The Yakushi-ji East Pagoda

An area with a secondary lean-to or pent roof, called a *mokoshi* ("skirt layer"), was added to each story of the east pagoda of the Yakushi-ji, so that from a distance the three-story structure appears to have six levels (pl. 1). According to records, the now lost two-story *kondō* also had a *mokoshi* on each level (a reconstruction with both *mokoshi* was completed in 1977), so that it too had twice as many roofs as actual stories; its beauty was praised by later generations as though it were a fairy palace. The east pagoda and the west pagoda opposite it (destroyed by fire in the early sixteenth century but now being reconstructed; pl. 67) were identical in appearance. Recalling Schelling's phrase "frozen music," the east pagoda is truly spectacular in the variety and rhythm of its architectonic forms. In contrast to the big, high, broad roof supported by three-stepped bracket complexes over the main core of each story, the *mokoshi* are tucked into the interspaces. The two *mokoshi* projecting from the wall plane

89

67. Restoration model of Yakushi-ji west pagoda.
(Nara Exhibition Hall of Japanese History, Kinki
Nippon Railway Building, Nara Station)

are supported by bracket complexes and surrounded by simple balconies. With both
the large and small eaves and the tightly contracted balconies arranged in three
stages, and with a leading role played by the straight lines of the rafters projecting
to the front, a rhythmical balance of remarkable beauty is produced. Consequently,
although the framework of this pagoda of only three stories would ordinarily appear
to be outlandishly high, it evokes no adverse reaction whatsoever; on the contrary,
we cannot but marvel at the feeling for plastic form that it exhibits.

Architecturally, the Yakushi-ji is a transitional monument between the Hōryū-ji
and the Tōshōdai-ji. In the three-stepped bracket system of the Yakushi-ji east pagoda,
there are no curved struts (*shirin*) as seen under the eaves of the later Tōshōdai-ji *kondō*,
but there is a small latticed ceiling (*noki-tenjō*) under the eaves; in contrast to the
kondō and pagoda of the Hōryū-ji, which without such *shirin* and ceilings have gloomy
recessed spaces under the eaves, the Yakushi-ji east pagoda, by means of the latticed
ceiling, gains a feeling of brightness and composure. At the Yakushi-ji, bearing blocks
and bracket arms are placed near the ends of straight tail rafters. The base rafters
are, as usual, straight beams, circular in section, and the flying rafters are square
and straight except that their under-surfaces curve up somewhat (pl. 70). In this
respect, the Tōshōdai-ji *kondō*, next in the evolutionary process, will exhibit a marked

90

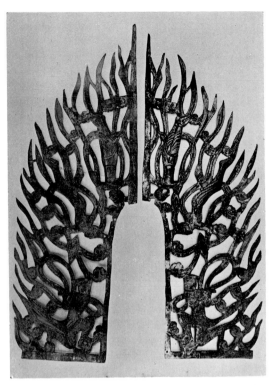

68. Flame decoration (*suien*) of finial, east pagoda, Yakushi-ji.

69. Second and third stories of east pagoda, Yakushi-ji.

stylistic change, to a completely curved eave form, which will become part of the light and exquisiste character of late Tempyō-period architecture (pls. 99–100). The east pagoda of Yakushi-ji still possesses the simple vigor of the earlier style in its details, and it is noteworthy that the building as a whole is free of the feeling of stiffness seen at the Hōryū-ji.

The style of the east pagoda of the Yakushi-ji is completely different from that of the Hōryū-ji, and yet, in comparison to other Tempyō buildings, it retains many aspects of earlier styles. For example, the projections called *zetsu* seen at the base of the Hōryū-ji cloud-shaped brackets are used for the last time at the Yakushi-ji east pagoda. Similarly, the scooped-out bracket construction (*sasaguri*) used at the Hōryū-ji, an ornamental device to give an appearance of greater strength to the upper bracket arm, continues in use in all post-Hōryū-ji Nara-period buildings, including the Yakushi-ji. By the Heian period, however, the form dies out.

Another example of continuity is related to building measurements and plans. As we have already said, it is known from the remains of the foundation of the original Yakushi-ji in the Fujiwara capital that the measurements and plan of its *kondō* and pagoda were the same as those of the new Yakushi-ji in the Heijō capital. When the temple was rebuilt at the Heijō capital, the other great temples abandoned old

91

70.   Detail of first story of east pagoda, Yakushi-ji.

temple styles, and there was a shift toward a new style of monastery building. Only Yakushi-ji follows the old standards. The most likely reasons for this are that the attachment of a *mokoshi* to each level was still a novel feature at that time, and that the builders had great confidence in the pagoda's architectural design. That the design of this pagoda was far above the ordinary is attested by the fact that in 1132, when Fujiwara no Michinaga began the building of the east and west pagodas at the Hōjō-ji, in Kyoto, they were in total imitation of those at the Yakushi-ji.

While we cannot prove that the Yakushi-ji east pagoda was a full reproduction of one at the Fujiwara capital, we do believe, for the reasons given above, that to a great extent the style of the end of the seventh century—the early T'ang style—has remained. However, although the present form of the east pagoda remarkably preserves the appearance of the original structure, the whitewashed walls that we see today on the *mokoshi* of each level were originally latticed windows, and the decorated metal fittings over the ends of the hip rafters and other rafters have disappeared.

71. Hokke-dō, Tōdai-ji.

OTHER EARLY TEMPYŌ BUILDINGS

Together with the east pagoda of the Yakushi-ji, Buddha halls which have survived
from the Tempyō regnal era (729–749) of the Tempyō period include Tōdai-ji's
Hokke-dō (Sangatsu-dō), the Yumedono in Hōryū-ji's east precinct, and Kairyūō-
ji's west *kondō*; also constructed around this time are Hōryū-ji's sutra repository and
refectory in the west precinct, great east gate, and Dempō-dō in the east precinct.

The Tōdai-ji Hokke-dō (Sangatsu-dō; pls. 71, 73, 91) was built around 746. This hall,
originally the *kondō* of the Kinshūzan-ji, predecessor of the Tōdai-ji on this site, has
at present an attached Kamakura-period worship hall (*raidō*), making it a deep building. The bracket complexes project only one step out from the wall to carry the eave
purlins. Both base and flying rafters are square-shaped. In the bracket system, the
bracket arms are slightly elongated, so that the well-extended eaves are securely
supported. Bracket complexes are not placed in between the wall purlins and the
long bracket tie-beams on top of the bracket arms as they are in later periods, but   93

72. *Ai-no-ma* (where Tempyō and Kamakura parts are joined), Hokke-dō, Tōdai-ji.

73. Hokke-dō interior, Tōdai-ji.

instead simple struts capped with bearing blocks (*kentozuka*; the same type of struts with bearing blocks are placed within the bays) are installed; the general impression is one of structural immaturity, recalling the simplicity of older architectural styles. Changes made by later generations include the removal of the interior floorboards (the floor is now of hard-packed earth) and the installation of latticework windows, but the original condition of the main section is well preserved. The *raidō* in front, built in the Kamakura period, was at first in the form of a double hall (*narabidō*), in which the main sanctuary and the *raidō* had separate roofs with a gutter in between to carry off the rain; but the two buildings were later put under one roof to give us the present structure. The gutter (pl. 72) still remains, however, to remind us of the earlier arrangement.

In 739, on the former site of Prince Shōtoku's palace, the monk Gyōshin built the Hōryū-ji east precinct, called Jōgūō-in, preserving in this name Shōtoku's title "Prince of the Upper Palace"; the Buddha hall of this precinct was the Yumedono (pls. 74–

94

74.   Door of west facade, Yumedono, Hōryū-ji.

75.   Yumedono interior, Hōryū-ji.

75, 88). On the roof of this octagonal hall is a splendid finial with base, sacred jewel, and a jeweled flask at the center resembling a relic pagoda. This signifies that, in addition to serving as a Buddha hall, this building was also a memorial pagoda for Prince Shōtoku. The support system is of the simple three-block type, mounted on an arm within the wall plane, and not projecting beyond it (pl. 76); the bracket arms are long, and the purlin-bearing bracket arms have the kind of molding common to Tōdai-ji's Hokke-dō (based on the reconstruction of the Yumedono; pl. 77).

A slight elongation of regular bracket arms and those on which purlins are placed directly, along with an overall expansiveness in feeling, are characteristic of early Tempyō architecture. Moreover, the purlin-bearing bracket arms with molding, which appear again for decorative effect after the Kamakura period (1185–1330), are seen in early architecture only at the Yumedono and Hokke-dō; this testifies to the fact that early Tempyō architecture had a youthfulness that had not yet fallen under the domination of a single style.

95

76. Yumedono finial, Hōryū-ji.

The Yumedono today shows an increase in the height of the bracketing system by the addition of one tier of bearing blocks in the Kamakura period, to extend the distance over which the eaves project. The appearance of the hall in earlier times was therefore simpler than it is today, and to that extent less heavy.

The west *kondō* of the Kairyūō-ji in Nara was probably built in 731 (pl. 78). It was extensively remodeled during the Kamakura period, and about all that remains today of the original form is the structure of the double tiers of the rainbow-shaped tie-beams, with frog-leg struts between them. The scale-model "miniature pagoda" in the Kairyūō-ji west *kondō* (pl. 79) is a work of fine craftsmanship, and accurate as a representation of the Tempyō-era architectural style. It has a triple-stepped bracket system similar to that of the Yakushi-ji east pagoda. Yet the bearing blocks have increased in number since the Yakushi-ji, and are arranged in orderly rows above and below one another (pl. 80); the *zetsu* (decorative projections of the bracket bases) have disappeared. The structure of the bracketing system has thus advanced one stage closer to that of the later Tōshōdai-ji *kondō*.

77. Restoration drawing of Yumedono, Hōryū-ji.

The sutra repository in Hōryū-ji's west precinct (pls. 81, 89) and its great east gate (pl. 82) are both typical Tempyō-period buildings, having three-block brackets and double rainbow-beams with frog-leg struts. Features held in common with Hōryū-ji's Yumedono and Tōdai-ji's Hokke-dō are the relatively large bearing blocks in relation to the size of the pillars, and the length and sturdy appearance of the bracket arms. The overall form of the sutra repository and the great east gate, both having ample but well-balanced proportions, is one of composed elegance.

The Hōryū-ji refectory (pl. 83), originally an administration building, is a utilitarian structure removed from the center of the temple compound. In keeping with its practical function, the refectory uses a bracket system consisting of a large bearing block and a single bracket arm (*daito-hijiki*)—that is, a simple bracket arm projects directly from the large bearing block in the direction of the wall plane and supports a beam without intermediate bracket arms with small bearing blocks; in the gable ends are simple double rainbow-beams without frog-leg struts; the interior uses the even more unpretentious construction of diagonal bracing (pl. 84). Even with

97

78.   West *kondō*, Kairyūō-ji.

a strictly functional building of this sort, however, the total impression is well ordered. Underlying this order is the meticulous care taken to create the basis for the eave curve by increasing the height of the pillars little by little toward the corner. Herein is clearly displayed the chief characteristic of Tempyō architecture—an emphasis on overall balance without undue attention to detail.

The Dempō-dō (pl. 90) was originally part of the residence of Emperor Shōmu's wife, Tachibana no Konakachi, and was later donated to Hōryū-ji. We know from this building that private residences of that time also used temple-style interior architectural features: the large bearing block with single bracket arm (*daito-hijiki*) and double rainbow-beams with frog-leg struts. As a residence the Dempō-dō had been built five bays long, of which the three rear bays were a room enclosed by walls and hinged doors; the front two-bay area was used as an open roofed area, and extending out in front of this was a wide veranda floored with wooden slats (pl. 86). When it was remodeled to become the lecture hall of the east precinct of the Hōryū-

79. Miniature pagoda, Kairyūō-ji.

80. Detail of miniature pagoda, Kairyūō-ji.

ji monastery, however, the Dempō-dō became seven bays long, as it stands today (pl. 87).

The light and gentle slope of the roof, and the stable articulate form created by the structure of the strong, stout framework, well expresses the character of Tempyō architecture, which is held in common by the buildings mentioned above. One important factor in achieving this effect is the moderation, by means of the horizontal elements, of the vertical flow of movement caused by the thickness of the upward-thrusting pillars—that is, the only structural horizontal members are the head tie-beams, joining one pillar to the next by being inserted into the pillar tops, and they are relatively thin; and the nonpentrating tie-beams (*nageshi*), which were added on after the main framework had been completed, are effectively low. Such small numbers of horizontal members, as well as their thinness and fine horizontal movement, are characteristic of this period, and the foundation for the lightness and smooth elegance of its architectural design is derived from such structural principles.

99

81. Sutra repository, Hōryū-ji.   82. Great east gate, Hōryū-ji.

83. Refectory, Hōryū-ji.

84. Refectory interior, Hōryū-ji.

85. Dempō-dō interior, Hōryū-ji.

86. Restoration model of Dempō-dō, Hōryū-ji.
(Tokyo National Museum)

87.   Dempō-dō, Hōryū-ji.

88. Yumedono, Hōryū-ji.
The Yumedono is the main hall of the Hōryū-ji
east precinct, built on the site of the Ikaruga
Palace of Prince Shōtoku. In 739, long after the
burning of Ikaruga Palace, the monk Gyōshin
built a memorial hall on the site, in commemora-
tion of Prince Shōtoku. Formally the precinct
was called Jōgū-in, and its main hall was the
Yumedono. The octagonal hall, more than the
usual Buddha hall, was considered a potent
design for praying for the salvation of the de-
ceased, and this intention was also displayed by
the splendid *roban* (square base) with *hōbyō* (a
bejeweled flask) placed on the rooftop. The main
image enshrined in the hall, the Guze Kannon
(ht. 179.9 cm.), is said to be the same height
as Prince Shōtoku. In the Kamakura period an
additional step was added to each bracket, with
the purpose of enhancing the structure's exterior
appearance. The eaves were also projected
farther than had previously been the case. In
spite of the repairs, much of the calm beauty
of the early period is preserved.

89. Sutra repository, Hōryū-ji.

The sutra repository is located on the west side of the semienclosed roofed corridor, just south of where the west and north sides of this corridor meet. Opposite is the belfry on the east. When they were first built the sutra repository and belfry stood outside and apart from the corridor, but when the lecture hall was rebuilt in the Heian period the corridor was extended to its present dimensions, jutting slightly inward, south of these two buildings, but nevertheless joining them. It is a type of high building construction (*yagura-zukuri*) in which the lower story is considerably higher than the lightly treated upper story, resulting in a neat and beautiful appearance. The construction of the double rainbow beams and frog-leg struts in the gable ends is an example of the Tempyō style, and shows that this building was constructed slightly later than those in the nucleus of the compound surrounded by the corridor.

90. Dempō-dō, Hōryū-ji.

The Dempō-dō was the lecture hall of the Hōryū-ji east precinct. Temple records state that it was presented to the monastery by Lady Tachibana, and had previously been her own residence. During the 1943 dismantling and repair, it was discovered that the seven-bay building was originally five bays, and that it was enlarged later, probably when it was transferred and converted from a residence into a monastery building. The wooden floor, unusual for a lecture hall, is a holdover from the original residential building. The Dempō-dō is a typical Tempyō-era structure with double rainbow beams and frog-leg struts over the core (*moya*), to which the *hisashi* are connected by tie-beams. The designs on the gable ends are a particularly lovely feature.

91. Hokke-dō, Tōdai-ji.
The ancient part of the Hokke-dō is the representative monument of the early Tempyō period.
Commonly called the Sangatsu-dō (Hall of the
Third Month), it was probably built in 746 on
the site it now occupies as a Buddha hall of the
Kinshūzan-ji, prior to the building of the Tōdai-
ji. In front of the five-by-four-bay main hall
there was, apparently from the very beginning,
a separate building or worship hall (*raidō*) with
a cypress-bark roof; but in the early Kamakura
period, 1199, the worship hall was rebuilt and
the roof connected to that of the main hall in the
form of a T, to create the complicated shape
we see today. The interior originally had a plank
floor, but the main hall has been remodeled to
the present earthen floor. The hipped roof
slopes gently and the deep eaves make a beautiful
shadow on the white walls. The exterior appearance is very Japanese in taste

6

TŌSHŌDAI-JI AND THE ARCHITECTURE
OF THE LATE TEMPYŌ PERIOD

The Building of Tōdai-ji

In the year 741, after the first stage of the Heijō capital building construction was finished, the emperor Shōmu issued an imperial proclamation commissioning the building of *kokubun-ji* and *kokubun-ni-ji* (official state-supported temples and nunneries) in each province throughout the land. The role of Buddhism, as the great moral and spiritual order which protects the nation, was increasingly strengthened, yet politically there was continuous turmoil. Emperor Shōmu, because of a rebellion against his regime, moved the capital again, at first to the Kuni capital in Yamashiro, near the modern Kyoto. Then he moved it to the Shigaraki Palace in Ōmi province (the modern Shiga Prefecture). But in 745, the seat of government was returned to its former location, the Heijō capital.

Amid the bewilderment and confusion caused by these moves, Emperor Shōmu ordered in 743 the construction of a colossal image of the Buddhist deity Vairocana, to be made of bronze and covered with gold leaf, and to serve at what must be called the headquarters of the national monastery system. Vairocana (Dainichi in Japanese) is the symbol of the basic generative force in the Buddhist cosmos, the source of all other Buddhas and, in fact, of all creation. The fabrication of the gigantic bronze image, as though an appeal to the saving compassion of the Buddha itself, can be seen as the embodiment of the fervent wish that political turmoil be brought to an end.

Work on the Great Buddha (Daibutsu) had begun at Shigaraki, but was not completed. Instead, when the seat of government was returned to the Heijō capital in 745, the project was shifted to the Tōdai-ji, the temple on the eastern edge of the city. Actual casting of the bronze plates out of which the image was assembled began in 747, and the statue, 10.82 meters high, was completed in 749. Three more years were needed to build the wooden hall, popularly called the Daibutsu-den (Great Buddha Hall), around the statue, and in 752 the lavish Eye-Opening Ceremony took place, dedicating the statue. Because there was no more land beyond the area occupied by the four great temples for such a grand compound, the Tōdai-ji was built outside of the capital, to its east, at the foot of Mount Mikasa. Modern research has determined that originally there was a hill of the same height as the Great Buddha at the location of the Daibutsu-den, and this great engineering task began with the leveling of the hill. The Daibutsu-den, which in the case of the Tōdai-ji is also the *kondō*, was eighty-seven meters across the front, fifty-two meters deep, and forty-seven meters high. In the Edo period the front was reduced to fifty-seven meters, and that rebuilding is as it now stands (pl. 94). Even in its present reduced state the building is the largest standing wooden structure in the world, so one can get an idea of the unparalled majesty of late Tempyō architecture represented by the original, much larger structure.

To the east and west and slightly in front of the Great Buddha Hall were a pair of seven-story pagodas, which were as much as one hundred meters high (pl. 95). To complete them took about twenty years. The two pagodas were probably finished around 764. Such splendid monastery structures are indeed testaments to a national effort.

The Tōdai-ji compound was frequently damaged by fire, and now the only Tempyō-period buildings which remain, apart from the Hokke-dō, are the Tegai Gate (pl. 96), the Shōsō-in treasure repository (pl. 93), the Tamukeyama Shrine treasure repository (pl. 98), and three other log storehouses (*azekura*). In the Kamakura period (1185–1330) one tier was added to the Tegai Gate bracket system, marring the original form. However, while the type of bracketing and gate construction is inherited from the early Tempyō period, the structure as a whole has a feeling of heaviness and strength, and in its grand scale the gate is reminiscent of the majesty of the Daibutsu-den itself.

Standard Architecture of the Late Tempyō Period

While the east pagoda of the Yakushi-ji is a continuation of the Hakuhō-period style, and the extant monument best typifying early Tempyō architecture is the Hokke-dō (Sangatsu-dō) of the Tōdai-ji, the building which represents the standard architectural style of the late Tempyō period is the *kondō* of the Tōshōdai-ji (pl. 97).

The Tōshōdai-ji monastery was begun in 759 by the T'ang priest Chien-chen (Ganjin in Japanese; 689–763) at the block at the fifth street, second avenue, of the right sector of the Heijō capital, on the site of the former residence of Prince Nitabe (pl. 61). It was not an official temple, but rather built with the help of aristocratic families converted to Buddhism. For this reason, the temple site covered only four plots of land, small in scale when compared to the twelve to fifteen plots of the four great temples of the capital. At that time the Tōshōdai-ji was a second-rank monastery, but it is extremely important now in that it contains the only remaining examples of a Tempyō-period lecture hall and *kondō*.

111

92. Kōfū-zō, Hōryū-ji.

The Kōfū-zō is a storehouse built by imperial order for the possessions of nobility. Its scale is equal to the Shōsō-in. The three bays to the north and south are used for storage and the center three bays are open. The north and south storage wings open onto the central open space to protect the doors from direct rainfall, so that the treasures could be moved without rain blowing in when the doors were opened. This arrangement is called the double storehouse (*narabi-kura*) style. A simple structure with plaster walls between the pillars, it is the only extant structure of its type. The important treasures of the Kōfū-zō are no longer stored there. Its exact date is difficult to establish, but it is more likely of the Heian than the Nara period.

93. Shōsō-in.

The Shōsō-in, the main storehouse of the Tōdai-ji, is located in the northern part of the monastery. Imperial treasures of Emperor Shōmu, collected from as far west as Egypt, were gathered there, and have been sealed in and preserved under the strict supervision of imperial decree since the eighth century. Two log structures are connected by a wooden plank enclosure, and one large roof is over the whole. In the central area, where there would normally be an open space [see pl. 92]), plank walls and a floor have been added, and chests containing the precious objects of the monastery are placed therein also.

94. Daibutsu-den, Tōdai-ji.

96.   Tegai Gate, Tōdai-ji.

95.   Restoration model of Tōdai-ji. (Tōdai-ji)

115

97. *Kondō*, Tōshōdai-ji.

The Tōshōdai-ji was founded by the Chinese monk Chien-chen (Ganjin) in 759, and the *kondō* built shortly afterward. Because Tōshōdai-ji was a small-scale monastery at the time, the *kondō* was not a two-story building, but a simple Buddha hall of a single story. It is the only *kondō* remaining from a Tempyō-period monastery. It was a new style of Buddha hall created in the Tempyō period, having a one-bay open porch across the front so that worshipers could approach the main images very closely. Light coming in through the high entrances fills the interior with brightness. When remodeled in the Edo period, the height of the ridge was raised 2.5 meters and the shape of the roof was changed to a steep incline which caused the upper part to appear somewhat heavy, with the consequent loss of the original lightness of Tempyō architecture. But the late Tempyō style is fully displayed in the perfection of the orderly arrangement around the eaves and in the massive framework.

117

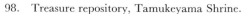

98.   Treasure repository, Tamukeyama Shrine.

   The *kondō* (pl. 97) is seven bays by four, measuring 28 by 14.6 meters. In front there is a one-bay-deep open porch that is defined by pillars across the front (pl. 100). This type of open-porch arrangement with supporting pillars developed in the Tempyō-style monastery after Kōfuku-ji initiated the use of a semienclosed roofed corridor attached to both sides of the *kondō* (pl. 64); it is the result of an attempt to relate the inner courtyard as a whole more intimately to the *kondō*, whereby the spacious courtyard could be used for devotional ceremonies. The Tōshōdai-ji *kondō* originally had such a corridor forming a courtyard in front, but it has not survived.

   The *kondō* employs the three-stepped bracket system normally reserved for buildings of the first rank during this period. It also has double eaves composed of circular base rafters and square flying rafters, standard in buildings of high rank. Yet, looking from the outside, one immediately notices that the bracket complexes are generally compact and reserved in comparison to the size of the building (pl. 99), a characteristic that is considerably at variance with early Tempyō-period architecture. The eave rafters curve up gently, and a calm beauty is apparent throughout. As for the details of the bracketing system (pl. 157), the bracket arm balanced on one bearing block and the curved-strut support (*shiringeta*) are placed at the second outward step

99.   Roof and eaves of *kondō*, Tōshōdai-ji.

of the bracket complex, strengthening the horizontal connection. There are now also curved eave struts, a feature not seen on the east pagoda of the Yakushi-ji. This orderly style running from rafters to curved struts, then to the thin wooden mullions of the little latticed ceiling in a continuous line, strengthens the feeling of stability of the eaves. The tail rafters also have a gentle curve. This style of three-stepped bracket complex continued without change until the so-called recent period (1573–1867) of Japanese history, about the only exception being development in the construction of the corners.

The front doors and the surrounding lattice windows in the Tōshōdai-ji *kondō* were originally higher than they are at present, giving a vertical feeling to the building, and the nonpenetrating tie-beams much thinner than the present-day framework, with its heavy horizontality that divides the building into upper and lower areas (pls. 102–4). Moreover, the ridge was originally about 2.5 meters lower and the incline much more gentle, giving the exterior of the building a far lighter appearance.

The Tōshōdai-ji *kondō*'s greatest distinction is that it presents an architectural form which is virtually complete in both design and structure, and it is here that we find the prototype of the native Japanese style (*wayō*).

119

120   100. Row of pillars of front bay, *hondō*, Tōshōdai-ji.

101. *Kondō* interior, Tōshōdai-ji. 121

102. Restoration model of *kondō*, Tōshōdai-ji. (Tokyo National Museum)

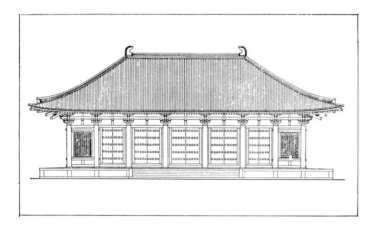

103. Restoration drawing of *kondō*, Tōshōdai-ji.

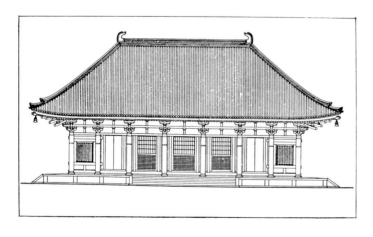

104. Drawing of present *kondō*, Tōshōdai-ji.

ESTABLISHMENT OF AN INTEGRATED TECHNOLOGY AND A CLASSICAL STYLE

The definite feeling of orderly stability in the Tōshōdai-ji *kondō* is quite different from the feeling of tension amid immaturity found in the Yakushi-ji east pagoda and the Tōdai-ji Hokke-dō. This difference is due to more than the full development of this style in the course of time; rather, we sense the firm establishment of a Japanese architectural taste, which was brought about in large part by the great construction project occasioned by the founding of Tōdai-ji.

The major stylistic differences between early and late Tempyō architecture can best be seen in the relative size of the bracket complex to the framework. In the later period, the bracket complex gradually became consolidated into smaller clusters; the strength of the early period is lost, and in its place is a stable feeling of order. We can gauge this change by comparing the length of the bracket arm to the size of the large bearing block (the latter is for the most part in proportion to the diameter of the pillar). Among the buildings employing three-stepped bracketing in the early Tempyō period, the proportion of the length of the bracket arm to the large bearing block of the Yakushi-ji east pagoda is 2.57:1; the Kairyūō-ji miniature pagoda is 2.20:1; and the Taima-dera east pagoda is 2.41:1. Of the later Tempyō-period buildings, the Tōshōdai-ji *kondō* is 2.00:1; the Gangō-ji Gokuraku-bō miniature pagoda is 1.93:1; and the Murō-ji five-story pagoda is 1.95:1. Thus the bracket arms of the later period are much shorter. Of the buildings using the three-block bracket system, the Tōdai-ji Hokke-dō and the Hōryū-ji great east gate are both 2.85:1, and the Hōryū-ji sutra repository is 2.77:1. Thus, the early Tempyō-period bracket arms are rather long, and later, as in the 2.35:1 proportion of the Tegai Gate of the Tōdai-ji, they are shortened. The scoop of the bracket arm, the feature which most expresses a bracket's power, is lost in the later period. It is not found in the Gangō-ji miniature pagoda or the Murō-ji pagoda of the last years of the Tempyō period, and this feature has disappeared completely by the Heian period.

Although, admittedly, it is difficult to say anything definite solely on the basis of assumptions from such a simple structure as the Tegai Gate, the only surviving later Tempyō-period structure at Tōdai-ji, there is no doubt that Tōdai-ji represents the turning point in the development of the standard architecture of the later Tempyō period. In the construction of the Tōdai-ji, craftsmen were brought together who had hitherto been competing with one another in the building of different temples, and in this way an exchange and integration of knowledge took place. At this juncture, the principal object became the creation of large-scale architecture by means of fixed methods that could be repeated in a regular way; this in turn gave rise to the need for technological simplification and stylistic uniformity.

Just before the construction of the Tōdai-ji, the order had been issued for the building of the *kokubun-ji* and *kokubun-ni-ji* (official state-supported temples and nunneries). When we examine the actual remains of the *kokubun-ji*, many of their pagodas were of a simple construction three bays wide, but they neglected to standardize the width

123

105. Miniature pagoda, Gangō-ji.

of the bays, which range from 3 to 3.6 meters (10 to 12 Tempyō *shaku*). Thus the Tōdai-ji, in response to the need for nationwide norms, was undoubtedly given the function of complying with a standardized plan. This was the stimulus for the creation of the Tōdai-ji style, which is also the style of the late Tempyō period, with its clarity, simplicity, and regularity—all in keeping with the Japanese taste in three-dimensional form.

From a description in the Shōsō-in archives, we can infer the original appearance of the *kondō* of the Jōdō-in of the Hokke-ji, built in 760 by the Tōdai-ji construction office, and in fact this *kondō* was very similar to the Tōshōdai-ji *kondō*. From this we can see that the Tōshōdai-ji *kondō* was in the Tōdai-ji style, and takes on even greater significance as the standard architecture of the late Tempyō period. We might say that, at this stage, the T'ang style had been thoroughly assimilated, and that Japanese architecture had advanced a step beyond faithfully copying Chinese architecture to the establishment of a classical style.

OTHER ARCHITECTURAL REMAINS

In addition to the above-mentioned structures surviving from the late Tempyō period, there are also the Taima-dera east pagoda (pl. 106), the octagonal hall of Eizan-ji (pl. 108), and the main hall (*hondō*) of the Shin Yakushi-ji (pl. 109), and remaining at the Tōshōdai-ji are the lecture hall, the treasure repository (*hōzō*), and sutra repository (pl. 111), the last two of which are in the *azekura* style.

The twin pagodas, east and west, of the Taima-dera, still stand (pls. 106–7). Although the east pagoda is judged to have been erected in the late Tempyō period, and the west pagoda somewhat after that, in the Heian period, stylistically they fall, respectively, into the early and late Tempyō period. Looking at the first story of each of these, we see that although there are no intercolumnar struts with bearing blocks (*kentozuka*) at the east pagoda, there are at the west. There, the distance between two bracket sets is too narrow to accommodate another bracket set, but wide enough to require additional support, which is provided by the intercolumnar struts. This difference is characteristic of the early and late Tempyō period, as discussed in the preceding section. At the east pagoda there is a bracket arm under the eave purlin which is made into a long member (*hakari-hijiki*) that extends to and adjoins the three-stepped bracket complex of the corner, a structurally more advanced system than that used at the late-Tempyō Tōshōdai-ji *kondō*, which uses intercolumnar struts; it is for this reason that the construction date of the east pagoda is not assigned to the early Tempyō period itself, but somewhat later. The first story of the east pagoda is divided into three bays, the plan decreasing to two bays in the second and third stories. Such a bold scheme offers an especially satisfactory sense of vitality peculiar to the early Tempyō period, and the total structure seems more compact as a result. In contrast, the west pagoda mechanically repeats the three-bay scheme in the upper stories, and the discontinuance of the practice of scooping out the upper surface of the bracket arm results in a loss of forcefulness; the difference between the styles of the early and late Tempyō period is evident.

The octagonal hall of the Eizan-ji (pl. 108) was built around 763. In form it is a plain, unadorned version of the Yumedono; the "sacred jewel" on top of the building is made of stone. The standard eight pillars in halls of this type have been reduced to four, and the bracket-arm scoop has been omitted from its three-block brackets. On the whole, it is a concise scheme.

The main hall of the Shin Yakushi-ji (pls. 109–10) is a low, serene hall which uses the simple large bearing-block and bracket-arm system (*daito-hijiki*). There is no decorative detail and even the interior is of the simple strut with diagonal bracing construction. It seems that originally the main hall was in its own precinct removed from the central part of the monastery. Its construction is assumed to have occurred sometime between the very end of the Nara period and the beginning of the Heian period. There is not much remodeling or reconstruction from later times, and the roof, especially, preserves the buoyancy of the time of its establishment. The simplicity of the Eizan-ji octagonal hall and the Shin Yakushi-ji main hall are decidedly suited

125

106. East pagoda, Taima-dera.   107. West pagoda, Taima-dera.

to Japanese taste, and this moderation in design became the keynote of later Japanese-style (*wayō*) Buddhist architecture.

The Tōshōdai-ji lecture hall (pl. 112) was moved in the mid-eighth century from its original location at the Heijō palace, where it was the Chōshū-den. It received extensive remodeling in the Kamakura period, which left only a trace of its Tempyō-period appearance in the style of the double rainbow beams of the interior (pl. 113).

The last major building project of the Nara period to be discussed here is that of the Saidai-ji, begun around 765 (pl. 114). None of the Saidai-ji buildings remain today, but according to the temple records, the ridges and eave ends of the *kondō* had a strong Chinese flavor, with relatively complicated affixed decoration. Rare three-colored glazed rafter-end cover tiles appeared in the excavations of the Saidai-ji west pagoda a few years ago (pl. 115).

126   In contrast to the *kondō*, the Saidai-ji Jūichimen Kannon-dō and the Shiō-dō,

108. Octagonal hall, Eizan-ji.

each placed in its own precinct, were double hall structures with cypress-bark shingled roofs. Called *narabidō* (twin halls placed one in front of the other with intervening open space between), this arrangement is purely Japanese. The temple as a whole was most likely based on the architectural style that became current after the construction of Tōdai-ji, and contrast with it was sought in decorative detail. This indicates that the importation of the classic T'ang style had reached its final phase.

The government enterprise of official temple building came to an end with the erection of Tō-ji and Sai-ji in Heian-kyō (modern Kyoto), the new capital since 794. Although these two temples served as symbolic Buddhist bastions for the preservation and pacification of the country, relations between the government and the Buddhist church had, by this date, so soured that their erection was merely a matter of form. There is also a hint here of the fact that as the government's former enthusiasm for Buddhism waned, architectural activity became torpid.

127

109.   Main hall, Shin Yakushi-ij.

110. Interior of main hall, Shin Yakushi-ji.

111. Treasure repository (left) and sutra
repository (right), Tōshōdai-ji.

112. Lecture hall, Tōshōdai-ji.

113. Interior of lecture hall, Tōshōdai-ji.

114. Remains of east pagoda podium, Saidai-ji.

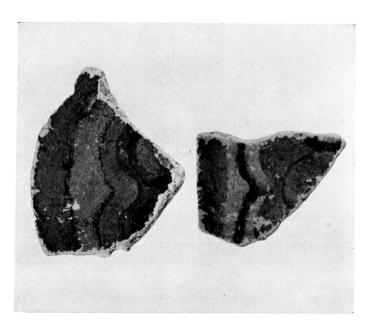

115. Excavated fragments of three-colored glazed tiles for rafter-tip decoration, west pagoda site, Saidai-ji. (Nara National Research Institute of Cultural Properties)

7

INTRODUCTION OF
ESOTERIC BUDDHIST ARCHITECTURE

A New Architectural Form

Political turmoil once more prompted the building of a new capital city. The piety of Emperor Shōmu's daughter, the empress Kōken, was so great that she came close to giving Japan a government dominated by the Buddhist priesthood. Conservative courtiers resisted her plans, and after her death in 770 they began preparing to move the seat of government to Nagaoka, only thirty kilometers to the north, in order to escape the powerful influence of the Nara monasteries.

Started in 784, work at Nagaoka was interrupted by an epidemic and ill omens. Another site nearby was selected, and in 794, when the basic elements of the imperial palace compound were complete, the government was transferred to the new city, called Heian-kyō, Capital of Peace and Tranquility.

In the early part of the ninth century, after the establishment of the Nara capital, Esoteric Buddhism, a religious ideology that had reached Sui China from India, was introduced into Japan. As its name implies, Esoterism (*mikkyō* in Japanese) was thought to be a doctrine so complex and intricate that it could be mastered only by a tiny number of gifted adepts, who transmitted it to chosen successors generation after generation. Esoterism placed great emphasis upon the spiritual and mental powers of the priesthood, who, for the sake of the faithful layman, conducted elaborate rituals intended to bring spiritual and material benefits, even Buddhahood itself, without delay.

Elements of Esoterism began arriving in Japan in the early Nara period, but in the sense of formally organized sects and a systematic theology, Esoteric Buddhism was introduced there during the first years of the ninth century, just a short time after the Heian capital was completed. Almost immediately a few monasteries of the Esoteric sects began to appear. On the practical level, buildings of a new form were created to accommodate the secret rituals and the congregation's relation to them. On the aesthetic plane, the new buildings reacted against the colossal, overpowering halls of Nara Buddhism by assuming an unadorned simplicity, one that did not necessarily require advanced technology or a new architectural style. Although the Heian period continued to follow the classical forms of the previous period, it also, with the

133

increasing construction of Esoteric Buddha halls, advanced the Japanization of temple architecture.

A special feature of Esoteric Buddhist architecture was the erection of monasteries at isolated sites in the mountains. There were also numerous mountain temples built in the Nara period before the introduction of Esoterism, the first known example of which is Sūfuku-ji in Shiga Prefecture. Built around 668 in the mountains at the command of Emperor Tenji, Sūfuku-ji is laid out in an arrangement similar to that of the Asuka-period metropolitan Kawara-dera. But such an arrangement is exceptional; the majority were small-scale private temples, having only a few halls and living quarters for the monks. With the increasing importation of Esoterism from China in the last years of the Nara period, monks began turning their backs on the splendor of Buddhism in the capital, and the number of mountain temples increased.

One of these was a small temple established by the monk Saichō (767–822) in 788 along the flanks of Mount Hiei, rising northeast above the plain where the Heian capital was later to be built. Called the Hieizan-ji, its central sector was a monastic

116.   Approach to main gate, Jingo-ji.

complex, the Ichijōshikan-in, containing a *yakushidō*, Monju hall, and a sutra repository. With their roofs covered with shingles made of cypress bark, each of these
small structures measured less than ten by five meters. In 805 Saichō returned from
China where he had absorbed the Esoteric doctrines of the Chinese T'ien-t'ai (Tendai)
school of Buddhism. Taking over the Hieizan-ji, he converted it into the headquarters
of the Japanese Tendai sect. It was also given a new name, Enryaku-ji, taken from
the regnal era in effect when he returned.

Saichō's friend and rival was the great monk Kūkai (774–835), who had also gone
to China but had studied a slightly different form of Esoterism. He returned in 806
to propagate the doctrines of the Shingon sect, whose headquarters, the Kongōbu-ji
(Kōya-san), he built in 816 atop Mount Kōya, in the mountainous heart of the remote
Kii peninsula in present-day Wakayama Prefecture. With the support of the imperial
court and the aristocracy, Kūkai also constructed buildings in 824 at the Jingo-ji,
atop Mount Takao near the Heian capital. In 836 he built the Kanshin-ji in Kawachi
province, east of present-day Osaka and a way station on the pilgrimage road to   135

Mount Kōya. In 823, the monastery of Tō-ji, inside the Heian capital, was also placed in his charge. The early Esoteric monasteries built during the lifetimes of Saichō and Kūkai, however, had barely gone beyond the planning stage and were small in scale. Two *hōtō* (a new style of pagoda which was circular with one square roof, built for Esoteric sect monasteries) were originally planned on Mount Hiei, dedicated to the preservation and pacification of the country, but only one was built, and even the great pagoda at Mount Kōya remained unfinished at the time of Kūkai's death.

The fully established Esoteric Buddhist monastery was clearly different from the Nara-period mountain temple, and the changes came about in the mid-ninth century, the generation of Saichō's and Kūkai's disciples. At Tendai monasteries were built *jōgyō-sammaidō* and *hokke-sammaidō* (halls for ritual circumambulation and the reading of the Lotus Sutra; pl. 133); halls dedicated to the Five Radiant Kings (*godaidō*) and the *kanjōdō* or purification halls were built at Shingon monasteries. Between 824 and 833, by the imperial command of Emperor Junna (r. 823–833), a *godaidō* and a *shingondō* (a hall for the recitation of the Mantras) were built at the Jingo-ji and, by 847, a *hōtō* was built. At the Tō-ji, the Kanjō-in was built around 843.

Emphasis was placed on these Esoteric Buddhist structures rather than on the *kondō* and lecture hall as formerly, and with the addition of topographical considerations, the traditional monastery arrangement, which revolved around the main halls in the center, became more dispersed in form. All religious buildings in early mountain temples like the Sūfuku-ji had roofs made of cypress-bark shingles; likewise, in the mountain temples of the Esoteric sects, main structures were roofed with cypress bark or wooden planks, as opposed to tile in the Chinese manner.

The buildings at the heart of the Esoteric sanctuaries were quite small, beginning with the Yakushi-dō of the Enryaku-ji and including the Kongōbu-ji *kondō* and the Jingo-ji Yakushi-dō and Gobutsu-dō. Each was a small hall of five lengthwise bays or less, with a cypress-bark roof. Probably the bracket systems were also abbreviated in structure, and the buildings, in general, extremely simple. The various new halls of Esoteric Buddhism were built with utmost concern for the rituals arising from the requisites of the faith; in order to conduct prayers and austerities, splendor and magnificence were altogether unnecessary.

From the standpoint of the technical virtuosity of Nara architecture, these buildings might be said to be of the second rank. But they appear on the scene as a new monastic type—dispersed throughout their mountainous and forested sites according to the topography, roofed with cypress bark, and imbued with the unadorned simplicity of the Japanese elements in their make-up.

Subsidiary Precincts (Betsu-in)

The cypress-bark roof is not the only new feature of Esoteric architecture which draws from native Japanese tradition. Others include the addition of a worship space (*raidō*) and the use of plank floors, which developed at the *betsu-in* (subsidiary precincts) of Nara-period monasteries. Designated by such names as *zen-in* ("meditation precincts") or *kara-in* ("Chinese precincts"), the *betsu-in* were independent enclosures located in one corner of the monastery compound and provided with their own dwelling and religious halls. In contrast to the life in the main part of the temple, with its emphasis on ceremonial, educational, and ritual activities, the monks in the *betsu-in* devoted themselves more to prayer, meditation, and austerity. The *betsu-in* thus had a residential character, and plank floors were used instead of the earthen floors in the conventional Buddha halls.

Also appearing in front of devotional halls of the *betsu-in* were the small, narrow structures called *hosodono* ("narrow halls"), built to provide a separate space for worshipers. For example, in the Tōzen-in (East Meditation Precinct) of the Yakushi-ji (built about 720) both a main hall and a *hosodono* were built, and in the east precinct of the Kōfuku-ji, in front of the 27-by-12 meter main hall (built around 761) a 27-by-6 meter *hosodono* was added; both *hosodono* had cypress-bark roofs. The Juichimen-dō and the Shiō-dō of the Saidai-ji had both expanded into double halls (*narabidō*) with cypress-bark roofs. Another way of building worship spaces was to place in front of a hall a *magobisashi*, an additional one-bay enclosed area attached to the building beyond the front aisle (*hisashi*). The small buildings of the Gangō-ji and Kōfuku-ji (all built around 770) had *magobisashi* worship areas with plank floors. The Tōdai-ji Hokke-dō, originally the *kondō* of the Kinshūzan-ji, had a worship hall (*hosodono*) at the beginning (later rebuilt), which also had plank floors. A parallel development probably took place in mountain temples; in short, because the *betsu-in* and mountain temples had a residential character, they took on some of the aspects of domestic architecture. Thus, with attachment of the worship space (*raidō*), a new, completely Japanese form of Buddhist building had already come into being in the Tempyō period, before the introduction of Esoteric Buddhism.

THE DEVELOPMENT OF RAIDŌ ARCHITECTURE

The Esoteric monastery, even if looked at solely from the standpoint of its emphasis upon special rituals and austerities, had much in common with the *betsu-in* and mountain temples. It was inevitable that it should not only make use of cypress-bark roofing, but eventually develop into a form possessing a plank-floored worship space (*raidō*) that was reflective of Japanese taste. The original Kanjō-in of the Tō-ji, for example, built in 843, was divided laterally into two parts. The main hall was seven-by-four bays; placed in front was the separately constructed *hosodono* ("narrow hall") of seven-by-two bays, to be used as a *raidō* or worship hall. The Jingo-ji Yakushi-dō (*circa* 830) also had a five-bay-wide worship hall. The developmental progression can be well understood at the Komponchū-dō of the Enrayku-ji (headquarters of the Tendai sect), where a *yakushidō*, Monju hall, and sutra repository were merged into

137

a single hall of eleven-by-four bays between the years 882 and 887, and a one-bay *magobisashi* was joined in front as a worship space.

During the repairs of the Komponchū-dō in 978 a second *magobisashi* was added to create inner and outer *raidō* each one bay in depth (pl. 117). The present-day Komponchū-dō is a 1640 rebuilding (pl. 118), but its style preserves the approximate appearance at the time of the 978 repairs, and gives us a good idea of the Tendai main-hall system of an inner sanctuary with hard-packed dirt floor and a worship space with plank floor. In summary we can say that although *raidō* architecture was outside the principal line of development in the Nara period, with the growing strength of Esoteric Buddhism it took possession of the architectural mainstream, and in the Heian period it accelerated and gave direction to the Japanization of temple architecture.

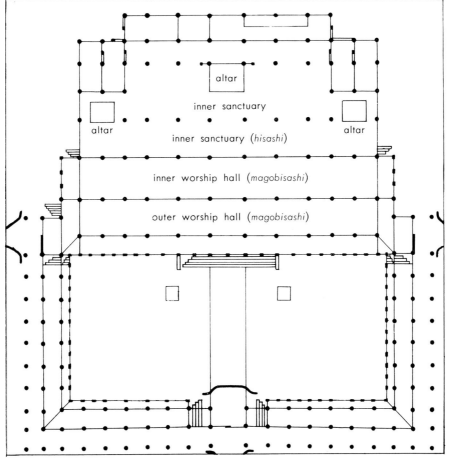

117. Old drawing of Komponchū-dō plan,
Enryaku-ji.

118. Komponchū-dō, Enryaku-ji.
The Komponchū-dō was built at Ichijōshikan-in within Hieizan-ji (the original name for Enryaku-ji), founded by Saichō around 789 on Mount Hiei. Being in the heart of the monastery, it was at first a temple consisting of three halls, which were later combined into one. The present structure is a 1640 rebuilding that follows the mid-Heian-period style of an eleven-bay hall with a roofed corridor attached. The Tendai sect main-hall style of plank floor in the outer sanctuary and a hard-packed earthen floor in the inner sanctuary can be seen here.

8

MURŌ-JI AND DAIGO-JI

The Heian period is the age of the classical Japanese modes of cultural expression: the short *waka* poem, the romantic tales of court life, calligraphy using the *kana* syllabary, and narrative scroll painting. In Buddhist architecture, only twenty-nine monastery buildings survive from the four hundred years of this era. About the same number of buildings, twenty-eight, remain from the one hundred or so years of the Nara period. Among the twenty-nine that remain from the Heian period, ten of them are Nara-period structures which, although rebuilt or extensively remodeled in the Heian period, follow, in style and form, the architectural tradition of the Tempyō period. Another eleven of these were made for the Pure Land Buddhist sect, which flourished from the eleventh century on, so that only seven of them are remains of Esoteric Buddhist buildings of the ninth and tenth centuries. As a result of the scarcity of architectural evidence, there are many unclear points about the actual appearance of early Esoteric Buddhist structures.

THE KONDŌ AND PAGODA OF MURŌ-JI

The Murō-ji, although not originally an Esoteric sect monastery, is useful to our study. Established at the end of the eighth century as a mountain temple of Nara Buddhism, it was not changed to the Esoteric Shingon sect until a later period. Of the original structures, only the *kondō* and five-story pagoda remain today. The *kondō* (pl. 120), a low, peaceful, small hall, uses the large bearing block with bracket arm (*daito-hijiki*), and its roof is of cypress bark. In the interior, a low wooden floor is built on sleepers laid directly on the ground, and the walls are made of wooden planks. In comparison to Buddha halls of a monastery built on a regular, flat site, this *kondō* is permeated with Japanese elements. A one-bay *magobisashi* was reconstructed in the Edo period as a worship space in front of the main hall. Measuring five bays by four, the main hall had a hip-and-gable roof at the time of building.

The five-story pagoda (pl. 122) is 2.4 meters square at the base of the first story, and the whole structure is only 16.2 meters in height, a tiny building. In comparison to the framework of the pagoda, the roofs are quite large, and a distinctive sense of beauty is

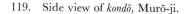

120 (page 144). *Kondō*, Murō-ji.
The Murō-ji was founded as a Shinto sanctuary between the last years of the Hōki era (770–781) and the beginning of the Enryaku era (782–806). The *kondō* and five-story pagoda remain from these times. The *kondō* is a Japanese-style Buddha hall with a finely shingled roof, and the interior has a low plank floor and board walls. Surrounded by trees and of harmonious simplicity in plan, it expresses a calmness quite different in spirit from the monastery plan on level ground. The front *hisashi* (worship area) was added in medieval times, and the present hipped roof was originally built in the hip-and-gable style; its outer appearance resembled that of the Yakushi-dō of the upper Daigo-ji.

121 (page 144). Taishi-dō, Kakurin-ji.
It is said that Kakurin-ji was founded by Prince Shōtoku, and that the Taishi-dō was built by him. But the present building, to the front and east of the main hall and in approximate opposition to a *jōgyōdō* (circumambulatory hall) to the west, was originally a *hokkedō*. It is known from a later inscription to have been built in 1112. A one-bay-square core is surrounded by one-bay *hisashi* on the four sides with an additional *hisashi* in front as a worship space. The style is a common one in late and post-Heian-period Buddhist structures that have a residential flavor.

to be seen in the repetition of the horizontally curving lines at the eave ends and in the gentle incline of the cypress-bark roofs. The increased curve at the ends of the tail rafters of the triple-stepped bracket system create a rather beautiful curved line (pl. 123). The base rafters and flying rafters are constructed with a much more gently sloping line than we see in the Tōshōdai-ji *kondō*. Moreover, the boldly scooped bracket-arm of the Nara period has disappeared. Instead, not only in the roof covering but also in the design of the details, we can see a modification of the architectural aesthetic, one that has greatly progressed toward the Japanese preference for quiet, orderly forms. *Kondō* and pagoda stand quite a distance from each other; enclosed by the cedar forests, they seem to be absorbed into their surroundings. This type of environment and architectural style undoubtedly represent that of the early Esoteric monastery.

120.   Caption on preceding page.

121.   Caption on preceding page.

122.   Five-story pagoda, Murō-ji.

This 16.2-meter-high pagoda, the smallest of the five-story pagodas, is traditionally said to have been built overnight by Kūkai. The successive diminution in size towards the top is comparatively slight, and the almost horizontal layers of the gently sloping cypress-bark roofs have a fragile beauty. The pagoda finial is unique be- cause it replaces the unusual type of *suien* (fili-greed metal ornament) with a "treasure flask" (*hōbyō*) on top. In spite of its small scale, surprisingly large timbers are used in the three-step bracketing system, and the other structural members are slightly thicker than those of the late Tempyō period. The entire form is imbued with exquisite delicacy.

144

123. Bracket system of five-story pagoda,
Murō-ji.

THE DAIGO-JI

From the end of the ninth century on, religious fervor spread and pious believers among the imperial family and aristocracy increased in number. Esoteric Buddhist monasteries came to be built on flat sites near urban areas as well as in the mountains. The Esoteric Buddhism that had reacted to Nara Buddhism and its ecclesiastical splendors was itself changed by aristocratic tastes. Removing themselves from the realm of rustic hermitages and tiny religious halls of the mountain temples, the Esoteric sects may have found it difficult to suppress a nostalgia for the large Nara-style monastic buildings. In 876 the Daikaku-ji, in 888 the Ninna-ji, and in 907 the Daigo-ji—all Esoteric monasteries on the outskirts of the Heian capital—were built by imperial command, and on a grand scale. Of these, the one whose original appearance is relatively well-known and some of whose structures have survived is the Daigo-ji.

The Daigo-ji was originally founded as a small mountain temple around 880 by the monk Shōbō. In the beginning it was a private temple, but in 907, Emperor Daigo made it his official place of worship, and a *yakushidō* and *godaidō* were built on the mountain at imperial command. Later, in 926, a monastery was begun on the plain at the foot of the mountain. In contrast to the completely Esoteric style of the religious buildings atop the mountain, the lower Daigo-ji was laid out in the Tempyō manner, recalling the Kōfuku-ji. The *kondō* (the body of the present building is Heian but the roof later) was built in the center and the five-story pagoda placed to the east, beyond the middle gate. With the exception of the pagoda and *kondō*, however, the other lower Daigo-ji buildings, which are not from the early period, have cypress-bark roofs, and the *kondō* has the Heian architectural feature of a narrow attached *raidō* resembling a *hosodono*. Today, the oldest surviving structures at the Daigo-ji are the five-story pagoda (pl. 124) of the lower section, completed in 951, and the Yakushi-dō of the upper Daigo-ji, rebuilt in 1121 (pl. 131), but following, it is thought, the early plan.

THE FIVE-STORY PAGODA OF DAIGO-JI

The Daigo-ji five-story pagoda (pl. 112) retains the standard three-stepped bracket system used from the Tōshōdai-ji *kondō* on, and for the most part follows the Tempyō style, but if we look closely, we see that a change has been made in the corner bracket complexes. The base rafters now function as independent supports which control the eave ends, and the structure of the framework places the load of the upper story directly on the tail rafters; but there is really very little technical progress in such minor improvements. In the interior, there is a low wooden floor and Esoteric Buddhist paintings on the walls and planks enclosing the central pillar (pls. 126–27); this is about the extent of the difference between this pagoda and the traditional one up to then.

124. Five-story pagoda, Daigo-ji.

The lower Daigo-ji monastery was built by the order of Emperor Daigo, the *kondō* constructed in 925, and the pagoda completed in 951. The height of the pagoda is 38.2 meters, and the first story is 6.7 meters square—the standard size for a five-story pagoda. The finial is especially high, about one-third of the height of the entire structure, and the nine rings are also large, resulting in an orderly and majestic appearance. It still transmits the late Tempyō style to a great extent, except for some development in the structure of the corner brackets. There is a low wooden floor on the first story. Buddha images taken from the Shingon mandalas and portraits of the eight patriarchs of the Shingon sect are painted on the interior walls and planks enclosing the central pillar of the first floor chamber.

125. Upper three stories of five-
story pagoda, Daigo-ji.

A suitable model to serve as a prototype for this five-story pagoda is said to have
been found at Fukō-ji, in Shiga Prefecture, probably a Nara-period temple. The overall proportions of the Daigo-ji pagoda are well balanced and the detailed, carefully
worked-out elements are refined. There is no feeling of dynamic rhythm like that
found in the east pagoda of the Yakushi-ji, but there is the beauty of system and order.
The difference reflects a loss of the healthy creativity of Tempyō architecture, and
shows that by this time builders were content simply to copy the perfected classic
styles and concentrate only on further Japanese refinements.

126. First-story interior of five-story pagoda, Daigo-ji.

127. Wall painting from five-story pagoda interior, Daigo-ji.

128. "Many treasures" pagoda (*tahōtō*), Negoro-ji.

OTHER ARCHITECTURAL REMAINS

The changes in multistoried pagoda architecture have thus far been shown to be slight, and the continuity between late Tempyō and early Heian forms clearly recognizable. One reason for this continuity may be that the single-storied *hōtō*, claiming its origins in the legendary Iron Stupa of Nagarjuna in South India, is introduced into the Esoteric monastery plan at least by the ninth century, and possibly in the eighth. The *hōtō* ("treasure" pagoda), or *tahōtō* ("many treasures" pagoda) when it has a *mokoshi*, is unique to Esoteric monasteries, especially those built in the mountains, and reaches its greatest popularity in the ninth and tenth centuries. Among present remains, the *tahōtō* of Negoro-ji, rebuilt at the end of the fifteenth century (pl. 128), retains the form of the early Heian period. At monasteries built on plains, however, from the Ninna-ji of 888 on, the multistoried pagoda of former times seems to have been preferable to the *hōtō* and spread to the mountain monasteries in the late Heian period.

One example of a multistoried pagoda at a late Heian-period monastery is the three-story pagoda of Ichijō-ji in Hyōgo Prefecture (pl. 129), erected in 1171. This is the oldest example of a pagoda with a wooden veranda around the first story. It will be recalled that in the Nara period a pagoda was built on a stone podium, and

129. Three-story pagoda, Ichijō-ji.

on the interior either a stone floor was laid or there might be one of hard-packed earth. At the tenth-century Daigo-ji five-story pagoda, the podium is constructed in the traditional way, but a low plank floor is in the interior. By the time we reach the late Heian construction of the Ichijō-ji pagoda, there was an important change to a *kamebara* podium (a hard-packed earthen mound covered with a kind of thick white plaster, shaped like a tortoise belly [*kamebara*]) with accompanying wooden veranda built around it. In that the pagoda was already perfected when it reached Japan, the introduction of such Japanese features came considerably later than it did for the temple halls.

Another noteworthy feature of the Ichijō-ji three-story pagoda is the use, in the support system on the first floor, of frog-leg struts (*kaerumata*) in place of intercolumnar struts capped by small bearing blocks (*kentozuka*). The oldest surviving instance of such intercolumnar frog-leg struts is found in the interior of the 1121 Yakushi-dō at the upper Daigo-ji (pl. 130), where, serving no structural purpose, they function as decorative detail. It is thought that, perhaps in the same way as the undulating bargeboards (*karahafu*), this decorative use derived from such objects of craftsmanship as the palanquin used for transporting a Shinto god, or the oxcart, a clumsy but highly embellished conveyance serving as a common mode of transportation for the courtiers of   153

130.　Yakushi-dō interior, Daigo-ji.

the Heian period. We can see from this that in the relative stagnation of architectural technique of the late Heian period, craftsmanlike delicacy came to play a central role in design concepts.

The style of the early Esoteric main hall is rather well transmitted at the upper Daigo-ji Yakushi-dō (pl. 116). Even though the present building is an 1121 rebuilding, it appears to follow the approximate scale of the 907 structure. Five bays by four, with a hip-and-gable cypress-bark roof, it is built on a podium made of rough uncut stones. The interior floor is hard-packed earth. The building is lower than the Murō-ji *kondō*, and large, wide eaves are supported by the gently sloping rafters, giving a feeling of tranquility. These rafters are nearly horizontal as they reach out, transforming the hitherto gloomy area under the eaves of earlier buildings by opening them up to the light.

The incline of the base rafters is closely related to a unique Japanese invention —the hidden roof (*noyane*), which flourished from about the tenth century on (pl. 16). The hidden roof was constructed above base rafters on which were placed struts that supported an additional layer of rafters. These are called hidden rafters because they are concealed from the exterior. After the hidden roof was invented, in order

to distinguish the two sets of rafters the term base rafter was replaced by the term visible or exposed rafter. With the hidden roof, not only was there a greater degree of independence of the exterior roof from the interior room space, and a concomitant freedom of spatial articulation of the inside, but the incline of the exposed rafters could be freely chosen. The eaves of the upper Daigo-ji Yakushi-dō show an important stage in the development toward the hidden roof (pl. 158). The visible rafters are below and, with struts on them, are positioned to carry the hidden rafters, or upper set, on which the cypress-bark shingles are laid. Unlike tiled roofs, in which individual tiles are bedded in a thick layer of clay laid on the upper surface of the roof framework, which is covered by some kind of sheathing, in cypress-bark roofs the shingles require a separate under-surface. The hidden roof probably developed from this specific constructional practice associated with cypress-bark shingles.

The tendency toward gently sloping eaves advances in proportion to the Japanization of temple architecture. We see in the Yakushi-dō of the Daigo-ji and the 1124 Konjiki-dō of the Chūson-ji (pl. 142) that in the last years of the Heian period the horizontal extension of the eave support (*kayaoi*) reached the ultimate position of being almost horizontal, increasing the brightness of the exterior as well as the refinement 155 of form. In contrast to the interior of the Murō-ji *kondō*, which at the time of building had an exposed-rafter roof (*keshōyane*; at present it has a latticed ceiling that was added later), thereby creating a high, empty space under the roof, in the Yakushi-dō at upper Daigo-ji a simple lattice ceiling was placed only over the inner sanctuary, where it was raised one step higher by putting one more tier of supports containing frog-leg struts and bracket complexes in line with the pillars surrounding this inner area. Formality and brightness were thus successfully combined in this interior space. In this respect, it can be said that, while the low height of the building and the earthen floors follow the unadorned early-period Esoteric main hall, the Daigo-ji Yakushi-dō reveals the results of the Japanization that had been in progress throughout the Heian period.

While the upper Daigo-ji Yakushi-dō follows the construction of an early period five-bay main hall, an example of the later arrangement of main hall with attached worship space (*raidō*) is found in the 1096 main hall of Ishiyama-dera (pl. 132). The present appearance indicates that the worship hall in front was rebuilt in the Momoyama period (1573–1614). The hip roofs of the main hall and worship hall are connected by a gable roof which has no gables, as the gable ends are attached to the hip roofs. The whole building resembles the letter I in plan. Since the worship hall existed from the beginning, it is thought that this structure was in the double-hall style. The main hall, though a rather large building, employs the simple three-block bracket system, and the fact that it has no special features is typical of Esoteric main halls. Built on a low foundation, the plank floor in the interior is also low, strictly according to Esoteric practice.

Another common structural type in Esoteric Buddhist architecture is the five-bay-square hall with pyramidal roof covered with cypress bark. It was traditionally used in halls for circumambulation (*jōgyōdō*), for the recitation of the Lotus Sutra (*hokkedō*), and for the recitation of the Mantras (*shingondō*). This tradition survives in the Enryaku-ji Jōgyō-dō and Hokke-dō (pl. 133) rebuilt in 1595. The only surviving Heian-period example, however, is the three-bay-square hall now dedicated to Prince Shōtoku (Taishi-dō) at Kakurin-ji in Hyōgo Prefecture (pl. 121), with its one-bay *magobisashi* across the front. The structure was originally built as a *hokkedō* in 1112. The three-bay-square *hokkedō* was the parent of the Amida hall which came into great popularity with the flourishing of Pure Land Buddhism in the eleventh and twelfth centuries. Several examples of square Amida halls with an attached *hisashi* serving as a worship area (*raidō*) survive from the last years of the Heian period. It is supposed that originally the *magobisashi* at the Kakurin-ji Taishi-dō was open. There is even some doubt that this area was part of the original structure.

A rather curious building is the Nageire-dō of the Sambutsu-ji (pl. 134), connected with a sect of ascetics who lived in mountain sanctuaries much as did the Tendai and Shingon sects. Dating from the twelfth century its form was introduced from Shinto shrine architecture, and is thus outside the scope of the present study.

132.   Main hall, Ishiyama-dera.

133. Jōgyō-dō and Hokke-dō, Enryaku-ji.

134. Nageire-dō, Sambutsu-ji.

9

THE HŌŌ-DŌ AND KONJIKI-DŌ

In the last phase of the Heian period, toward the last century of the long Fujiwara epoch (898–1184), we see a reemergence of brilliant color in temple architecture. Different, however, from the assertive, grandiose, brightly colored forms of Tempyō architecture, derived from T'ang China, the Fujiwara was an especially decorative style of architecture, endowed with the subtleties of Japanese taste, and while it advanced the Japanization of building style, it also created a unique sense of beauty. This was the architecture of Pure Land Buddhism, in which the Amida hall was of central importance.

MICHINAGA'S BUILDING OF HŌJŌ-JI

The great patron of Pure Land Buddhist architecture was the Fujiwara family, and the greatest of the Fujiwara patrons was Michinaga (966–1027), who, although never appointed chief advisor to the emperor, was regent in all but name. His constructing the Hōjō-ji on the edge of the Heian capital produced forms of temple architecture never seen before, truly an epoch-making event. The Heian-period temple projects of the Fujiwara family had actually begun with the 924 Hōshō-ji of Tadahira (880–949), who had brought his family to a new plateau of power and influence, followed by Tamemitsu's Hōjū-ji (988) and Kaneie's Hōkō-in (991). They continued steadily until the time of Michinaga, who, a most pious Buddhist, performed many benefactions, including the construction of the Jōmyō-ji in Uji, south of Kyoto, in 1005. Projects of the Fujiwara family flourished in alternation with those of the imperial household, which from the beginning of the tenth century onward had commissioned such monasteries as the Ninna-ji and Daigo-ji—thus promoting a vast amount of architectural activity.

Michinaga began building the Hōjō-ji in 1019 on a 240 m.² site on the west bank of the Kamo River, just to the east of his residential palace. The monastery (pl. 135) was arranged with a sutra repository and belfry flanking a central *kondō*, with a *godaidō* to the east, a *yakushidō* to the southeast, a *jissaidō* (a hall for purification ceremonies held ten days of each month) to the west, and an Amida hall to the south-

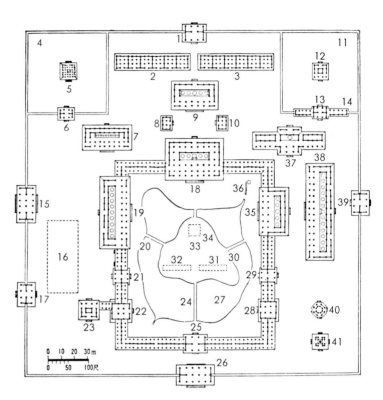

135. Assumed plan of Hōjō-ji (after Fukuyama Toshio): 1) great north gate. 2) monks' quarters. 3) monks' quarters. 4) northwest precinct. 5) Jōgyō-sammaidō. 6) middle gate. 7) Jissai-dō. 8) belfry. 9) lecture hall. 10) sutra repository. 11) northeast precinct. 12) Jōgyō-sammaidō. 13) middle gate. 14) semienclosed roofed corridor. 15) great west gate. 16) Amida hall after 1025. 17) great southwest gate. 18) kondō. 19) Amida hall. 20) west bridge. 21) middle west gate. 22) belfry. 23) Hokke-sammai-dō. 24) south bridge. 25) middle south gate. 26) great south gate. 27) pond. 28) sutra repository. 29) middle east gate. 30) east bridge. 31) dressing room. 32) dressing room. 33) island. 34) stage. 35) Godai-dō. 36) spring. 37) Shaka hall. 38) Yaku-shi-dō. 39) great east gate. 40) octagonal hall. 41) pagoda.

west. In the center a pond was dug with an island in the middle. Directly south of the pond was the south middle gate, and a larger great south gate was on the same axis beyond it. In addition to the lecture hall, Śākyamuni hall, Hokke-sammai-dō, five-story pagoda, octagonal hall, and Shingon-dō, there were *betsu-in* in the northeast and northwest with *sammaidō* as the main hall for the performances of circumambulation ceremonies. The splendor of the ensemble is described in the *Eiga monogatari* ("Tales of Glory" of the Fujiwara family covering the period 888–1092) as "even like that of the Pure Land itself."

Pure Land Buddhism flourished in Japan from the mid-tenth century onward, and although a central aspect of the faith was the requirement that the devotees contemplate upon Amida (Amitābha) Buddha, Lord of the Western Paradise, through meditation and recitation of his name, noble families like Michinaga's were not content with simply concentrating spiritually upon Amida's Paradise; they created in this world an intimation of the magnificence of the next, a magnificence to which they became addicted. At Michinaga's vast Hōjō-ji, the first structure to be completed was the Amida hall (Muryōju-in) of 1020. Oriented to the east, it was divided into   161 eleven bays in order to provide for the installation of nine separate statues of Amida, symbolizing the nine sectors of his Paradise where the faithful are to be reborn. Rebirths in the nine sectors were depicted in paintings on the interior doors and walls. Elsewhere in the interior were inlaid ornaments of mother-of-pearl and semiprecious stones, and in the front central part was the place where Michinaga himself performed his recitations.

The other buildings at the Hōjō-ji, beginning with the *kondō*, were done in the Esoteric Buddhist tradition, but these were made rather to fulfill the formal requirements of a monastery, the real center of faith being the Amida hall. In addition, Michinaga built within the temple grounds a five-bay residence of the *shinden* type, as though he were actually living in the Pure Land as a consequence of his piety. Even though the Hōjō-ji was called a temple, it was actually a private residence; the arrangement of the buildings around a central pond has much in common with the *shinden* style of domestic architecture used for the country estates and town houses of the Heian-period aristocracy (pl. 136).

In 1058, just after its completion, the Hōjō-ji was destroyed by fire. Soon afterward, it was rebuilt, but it was destroyed again in the early Kamakura period (1185-1330). Today, the temple site lies within the banks of the Kamo River and of its

136.   Model of *shinden-zukuri* residence.
(Kanagawa Prefecture Museum)

original appearance nothing remains. Yet from records we know of the impressive splendor of its halls, which equaled that of the later Hōō-dō of the Byōdō-in and the Konjiki-dō of the Chūson-ji. It was at the Hōjō-ji, in the magnificence of its use of color and mother-of-pearl, that the model for the elegance of Pure Land Buddhist architecture was conceived. By the end of the Heian period nearly thirty Amida halls for the installation of nine statues of Amida had been built, each of which is known from records, but the earliest example of this type of Amida hall was that at Hōjō-ji.

THE HŌŌ-DŌ OF THE BYŌDŌ-IN

The Hōjō-ji, fruit of the power and authority of Fujiwara no Michinaga and his son Yorimichi, cannot be seen today, but a structure comparable to it can be seen in the Hōō-dō (or Phoenix Hall) of the Byōdō-in (pls. 137, 139).

   The Byōdō-in, originally a resort villa on the banks of the Uji River, was converted by Michinaga's son, Yorimichi, into a temple in the year 1052. In that year the main hall was dedicated, and the Hōō-dō in the following. The Hōō-dō is the popular name for the Amida hall, the only major structure of the Byōdō-in to survive in good condi-   163

137. Hōō-dō, Byōdō-in.

tion. It is one of the most extraordinary buildings in the history of East Asian architecture. The middle hall consists of a central core (*moya*) measuring three-by-two bays with surrounding *mokoshi*, so that from the exterior it seems to have two stories. It is the focal point of the building and encloses the primary object of worship, a wooden statue of Amida 2.84 meters in height. Flanking this central hall are two wings, L-shaped in plan and two stories high, which are provided with turret-towers at the corners. From the back extends a taillike covered corridor. This unusual shape, it is thought, was copied from Amida's jeweled palace in paintings of the Western Paradise, the so-called Jōdo mandala. Its style could also be seen in the layout of the Great Hall of State of the Heian imperial palace. In fact, the composition of the palatial structure where the Buddha Amida dwells as lord became, so to speak, an ideal for domestic architecture of the time, pervading even the *shinden* style of building. This epoch-making style became a model from that time on, and the Shōkōmyō-in, a temple erected by the retired emperor Gotoba in southern Kyoto in 1136, and the Muryōkō-in in Hiraizumi of about 1170 were modeled on it.

In the center of the hall an exquisite canopy of filigree-carved wood was suspended (pl. 138); other wooden members—the pillars, bracketing, and ceiling—were decorated in beautifully colored designs; and scenes of Amida coming to welcome the dead into the nine levels of Paradise were painted on the interior doors and wall panels. On the altar were decorative floral patterns of inlaid mother-of-pearl, and in this way a realm of exquisite elegance was created around the central golden Buddha image.

The structure of the middle hall, with its use of triple-stepped bracket complexes along with circular base rafters and square flying rafters to form the eaves in the old style, inherits the traditional technology for Buddha halls coming down from the Nara period. It is true that the corner bracket complexes, which had been improved upon, little by little, from the time of the east and west pagodas of the Taima-dera to that of the pagoda of Daigo-ji, were finally brought to perfection at the Hōō-dō, but otherwise the basic structural system is almost entirely traditional. However, the pillars, bracket complexes, and even the rafters of the *mokoshi* all have broadly chamfered corners (called *ōmendori*), a feature which is not seen prior to the Heian period. The fine design of the *mokoshi* alleviates the heaviness of the main building, and a beautiful overall harmony is achieved.

As we have already seen at the Daigo-ji, in the large-scale buildings of the late Heian period handsome temples were selected from already existing structures to serve as models. The Hōjū-ji octagonal hall (Hakkaku Endō), for instance, was built in imitation of the octagonal hall (Nan'en-dō) of Kōfuku-ji. In this way, the aestheticism and refined taste of the Heian aristocracy gave birth to such beautiful buildings as the Hōō-dō.

It is well worth noting, however, that the refined elegance of Fujiwara-period architecture is, fundamentally, in no way due to thinness of members or frailty of appearance. Since there were no major structural developments during the Heian period, and the only possible exception to this, the hidden roof construction, did not go beyond playing a secondary role that allowed the slope of the exposed rafters to be freely changed, there was thus no essential difference from the architecture of the Nara period. For this reason, the size of the wooden members could not be made as thin as they were to become from the middle ages on with the improvement of penetrating tie-beams (*nuki*) and joinery (*shiguchi*) as well; rather it was necessary to keep them thick and heavy. In the Nara period, nonpenetrating tie-beams (*nageshi*) were used above and below doors and windows, and as their effectiveness as structural connectives between pillars was recognized, they were gradually made thicker; by Fujiwara times they had reached an ungainly size in comparison to the thickness of the pillars. Likewise, the shape of the head tie-beams had been nearly square in the Tempyō period, but by the Heian period they were, in cross section, heightened to a rectangle; accordingly, the clarity of Tempyō-period building frameworks, 165 made up of sturdy pillars rising in clean vertical lines, was lost, as horizontal beams came to be thicker and obscured the vertical movement of the pillars, resulting in a heavy appearance. And as in the process of Japanization buildings became lower, there were cases in which the outward appearance was squat and ponderous. However, despite the clumsier proportions of structural members, the entire building had an elegant appearance due to the skillful techniques for chamfering edged timbers and creating gently curved members as well as to the delicate use of lacquer and color in accordance with the refined taste of the Fujiwara aristocracy. The significance of the Hōō-dō lies in its bringing the harmony between architecture and surface decoration to the highest level. Later, the dependence upon decoration became stronger and the refinement of architectural forms conversely became weaker.

The rear bays of the side facades of the Hōō-dō are now enclosed with plank walls, but when it was first built there were doors here as well as in all the other bays, so that the main core (*moya*), three bays wide by two bays deep, could be opened on all sides. The *mokoshi* has a fine, wood slat floor, and the top of the foundation is paved with square stone slabs, an unusual technique, and we see once again the refinements that create the buoyant atmosphere of the *mokoshi*.

FLOURISHING OF AMIDA HALL ARCHITECTURE

The decorative effects seen at the Hōō-dō progressed to the point where the entire structure became a work of craftsmanship, and this stage was reached in the Konjiki-dō of the Chūson-ji at Hiraizumi (Iwate Prefecture) in the north of Honshu.

When government control by the Fujiwara regents ended, and the period of government by cloistered emperors commenced, the emperor once again replaced the Fujiwara family as the focus of temple building activity. Beginning with Emperor Shirakawa's Hōshō-ji in 1077, there was an unprecedented architectural boom in the capital from the last quarter of the eleventh century to the first half of the twelfth. The Pure Land sect spurred this activity through the concept that religious virtue could be amassed through the patronage of Buddhist statues and pagodas. It is recorded that in his lifetime Emperor Shirakawa commissioned the building of 127 colossal statues of the Buddha (standing figures 4.84 meters high, seated figures half that), 6 statues of half this size, 3,150 lifesize Buddha statues, and 2,930 images of less than 90.9 centimeters, in addition to 21 halls and pagodas. The erection of numbers of Amida halls, as aristocratic donations, at temple sites like the Hōkai-ji and Daigo-ji is also recorded.

This spirit in the capital spread to the various provinces, and the building of Amida halls flourished throughout the country. In particular, in remote Mutsu province (Iwate Prefecture) in northern Honshu, a provincial branch of the Fujiwara rose to power and wealth, and beginning in the early twelfth century undertook the construction of temples on a considerable scale around Hiraizumi, their capital.

139. Hōō-dō, Byōdō-in.
The Byōdō-in, originally a villa along the banks of the Uji River, was converted into a temple by Fujiwara no Yorimichi, son of the illustrious Michinaga. Its Amida hall was built in 1053. It is unclear whether this Amida hall received the name Hōō-dō (Phoenix Hall) because both ends of the ridge are decorated with phoenixes of gilt bronze, or because the plan of the structure itself is similar to the shape of a bird, with the central hall (*chūdō*) as its body and "wing" and "tail" corridors attached. Befitting its name, it possesses a beauty rich in variation. The interior is all the more splendid with its colorful designs, devotional paintings, and mother-of-pearl inlay. This famous structure was created by the Heian aristocracy for help in attainment of the Paradise of the Pure Land.

Led first by Kiyohira (?–1128), these provincial Fujiwara lords built large, expensive temple compounds over a seventy-year period. The first project undertaken was the rebuilding of an old temple, the Chūson-ji, to which was added an artificial pond even though the temple was located in the mountains; next was the Mōtsu-ji, which was built completely facing a pond, as were others—the Kanjizaiō-in and the Muryōkō-in. And all were made in emulation of the style of the Heian capital. The great temples built in the Heian capital at the end of the Fujiwara period have disappeared; even their remains have not been accurately established. But at Hiraizumi, the Chūson-ji's unique mortuary hall, the Konjiki-dō, and the foundations of the Mōtsu-ji have been preserved, and from these we can imagine the appearance of the lost temples of the capital (pls. 140–41).

THE KONJIKI-DŌ OF CHŪSON-JI

At Chūson-ji, in the year 1126, noble families from the Heian capital recited the prayers of a dedicatory service, marking the renewal of the temple. The new compound, built in emulation of the style of the Heian capital, consisted first of all of the square *kondō* with a three-by-three bay core, surrounded by a *hisashi* on all four sides. There was also a sutra repository, two stories high, along with a three-story pagoda, a two-story Amida hall (the Daichōju-in, or Daidō), and a Śākyamuni hall. In the garden pond floated dragon-headed boats recalling the splendid days of the Chinese Han palaces.

The most celebrated part of the temple today, as well as the only remaining structure from the Hiraizumi Fujiwara era, is the tiny structure built in 1124 and called the Konjiki-dō. Its plan, containing a one-bay-square sanctuary with *hisashi* surrounding it on all sides, is characteristic of almost all Amida halls of this period (pl. 142). The pillars which surround the inner sanctuary, as well as the lintels and bracketing, are decorated with inlaid mother-of-pearl, and gold leaf was applied to the walls of the outer sanctuary as well as to those of the exterior. For preservation the hall was recently placed in a concrete building and encased behind glass.

The principal Amida hall of the Chūson-ji compound was the Daichōju-in, which housed an enormous central image (approximately nine meters high) with four smaller statues on either side, making it a so-called nine-image Amida hall. The Konjiki-dō serves as a mortuary chapel: the mummified bodies of three Fujiwara nobles are interred under the three altars within. Its ornamentation is virtually the same as that of the Hōō-dō, both temples making full use of the elegance of craftsmanship of the day. At the Konjiki-dō the observer is astonished at such splendor, but the architectural details are surprisingly rough and without subtlety. The structure itself has become secondary to the display of the skill of the lacquer artists. The refined elegance of the Hōō-dō is lost, and has been replaced by a certain structural stolidity, indicating the condition of Fujiwara-period architecture in its final phase.

140.   Garden at Mōtsu-ji.

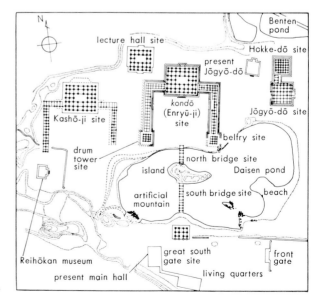

141.   Mōtsu-ji monastery plan.

142. Konjiki-dō, Chūson-ji.
Among the many temples built in Hiraizumi in the Kyoto style by a powerful
branch of the Fujiwaras in the north-
eastern half of the main island of
Honshu, the Chūson-ji, erected by Fujiwara no Kiyohira, was the largest in
scale. The Konjiki-dō, or Golden-colored
Hall, was a small one-bay-square Amida
hall built on a hillside at the back of
the monastery grounds. According to an
inscription on a ridgepole, it was built in
1124, and Kiyohira and his wife were
the patrons. The carpenter was named
Mononobe no Kiyokuni. Although it is
a small hall, gold leaf is used around the
sides both inside and outside, and in the
inner sanctuary the pillars, nonpenetrating tie-beams, and bracketing are decorated with Buddhist images covered with
lacquer filled with gold dust as well as
floral patterns done in mother-of-pearl.
It had been protected by a structure
built over it fairly soon after it was first
constructed, but during the recent total
repair and restoration this protective
building was replaced with one made of
concrete and the Konjiki-dō was itself
encased in glass to preserve the delicate
lacquer and gold leaf.

143. Konjiki-dō interior, Chūson-ji.

OTHER REMAINING AMIDA HALLS

There are other Amida halls surviving from the late Heian period demonstrating the structural variations of this basic sectarian building type. Located in the southern hills of Kyoto Prefecture, for example, is the Jōruri-ji, whose main hall (pl. 145), built in 1107, is the only nine-image Amida hall surviving today. Quietly overlooking a lotus pond, it has the composed appearance of a garden structure of a mountain villa. The exterior is exceedingly plain, the only bracket complex used being simple boat-shaped bracket arms (*funa-hijiki*) at the corners only. Inside the hall (pl. 144), a particularly high ceiling is raised only over the one-bay-square central area enshrining the main image. That the deft organization of interior space can also be seen derives from the development and use of the hidden roof construction. In 1178 the Jōruri-ji three-story pagoda (pl. 146) was moved from its Ichijō-Ōmiya site in the capital, Heian, to its present site on the hillside facing the pond. The thin-timbered, delicate appearance of the pagoda is suitable to its use at a Pure Land temple.

The main hall of the Sanzen-in at Ōhara, north of the city of Kyoto, was built around 1148, and is known for the unusual ceiling raised over the inner sanctuary, resembling the bottom of a boat (pl. 147). The main hall is a tiny three-bay-square building cleverly constructed to enshrine large wooden statues of Amida and two flanking bodhisattvas, which, in the small space, are viewed close at hand. Moreover, the altar platform in the inner sanctuary is raised only one step higher than the outer sanctuary, strengthening even more the sense of familiarity between worshiper and image, and reminding us of the purity and intensity of people's devotion to the Pure Land at that time. Today, only the inner sanctuary has survived from early times; the surrounding *hisashi* that comprises the outer sanctuary is so much restored that it is considered new.

Although most provincial Amida halls surviving today are only three bays square (a one-bay-square inner chamber surrounded on four sides by a one-bay *hisashi*), they are nonetheless rather large. The 1160 Ganjō-ji Amida hall in Fukushima Prefecture north of Tokyo is known by the popular name of Shiramizu Amida-dō (pl. 148). The single-step brackets and the wide, overhanging eaves imbue the hall with a grave, imposing elegance, in whose details may be found the style of the capital (pl. 149). The hall was originally built on an island in the center of a pond, but now most of the pond has been filled in.

The Daidō (Ō-dō) of the Fuki-dera on the Kunisaki peninsula in Ōita Prefecture (pl. 150) is also of the basic Amida hall type, but the worship area in front has been deepened, making the structure rectangular in plan. To conceal the fact that the hip rafters are placed in front of the pillars of the inner sanctuary, rather than over them as was the norm, a finely latticed, coffered ceiling was erected over the entire *hisashi*, creating a tranquil interior space. In the Nara period, ceilings were built in a construction called a *kumi-ire tenjō*, a latticed ceiling in which thick timbers closely tied to

144.　Interior of main hall, Jōruri-ji.

the framework were placed in a grid pattern (pl. 101). The ceiling of the Hōō-dō in the Heian period follows this tradition, but with the development of the hidden roof construction that permitted the installation of a ceiling unrelated to the roof structure, there appeared a new type of coffered ceiling, with a finely latticed pattern within each coffer, that complemented the simultaneous increase in the delicacy of interiors. It is as if the design of the canopy of the Hōō-dō were enlarged to fill the entire interior of the hall. This method became a major element in buildings of the native Japanese (*wayō*) style in the middle ages, and the ceiling of the Fuki-dera Daidō is an example. However, surprisingly large timbers are used in the Daidō for such structural members as pillars and nonpenetrating tie-beams, the bracket and bearing block complexes, rafters, and so on; in contrast to the fineness of the ceiling, they produce a slightly incongruous feeling, indicating one of the limitations of Heian-period architecture— the fact that the structural techniques of the framework lagged behind roof structure and ceilings. Clearly, the Japanization of architecture was not a simple process.　175

145.   Main hall, Jōruri-ji.
The Jōruri-ji was an ancient temple rebuilt in 1097 by the monk Gimei, and at the end of the Heian period this monastery surrounding a pond assumed its present appearance. Its main hall is an eleven-bay building enshrining nine images of Amida Buddha arranged in a row, each occupying its own bay. It is said that this hall, built in 1107, was moved in 1157 from the opposite side of the pond to its present site. It is a simple hall, with boat-shaped bracket-complexes used only at the corners. The Jōruri-ji main hall is the only remaining nine-image Amida hall of the many built at the time.

177

146. Three-story pagoda, Jōruri-ji.

147.   Interior of main hall, Sanzen-in.

148. Shiramizu Amida hall, Ganjō-ji.

149. Interior of Shiramizu Amida hall, Ganjō-ji.

150. Daidō, Fuki-dera.

The Hōkai-ji Amida hall, in Kyoto (pls. 151–52), was rebuilt during the early Kamakura period. The existing hall is one-bay square, surrounded by *hisashi* on four sides, but built on such a large scale as to produce a five-bay plan. Moreover, the installation of a *mokoshi* has made it appear from the outside as if it were multistoried. The present *mokoshi* has been made into a porch or loggia open on all sides. In the original, the rear half was divided into a number of small rooms where devotees might retire in prayer. For these special features, this building may be considered one type of Amida hall.

Structures like this are comparatively simple on the outside, but on the interior they reveal the special character of Fujiwara-period architecture with its fondness for subtle decorative effects: the brightly colored Buddhist images and design motifs on the pillars and ceilings, and the walls adorned with scenes of paradise and divine salvation. However, the Amida hall of the Kōzō-ji in Miyagi Prefecture, built around the mid-twelfth century, is different (pl. 153). The standard three-bay-square type, it is covered with a thatched roof made of miscanthus reed, and in its simplicity of form is completely without color. The interior is dominated by a 2.8-meter image of Amida Buddha, which, together with the large size of the timbers, produces a feeling of boldness. Thus, in provincial areas there were also Amida halls imbued with an austere vigor far different from the taste of the capital.

151. Amida hall, Hōkai-ji.

152.   Interior of Amida hall, Hōkai-ji.

153.   Amida hall, Kōzō-ji.

IO

BIRTH OF THE MEDIEVAL MAIN HALL

Development of the Hidden Roof Structure

As Heian-period architecture progressed in its process of Japanization, builders came to prefer such materials as cypress bark for shingles or wooden planks for roofing. In response to the requirements of building function came the worship hall (*raidō*) and the wooden plank floor. The technical innovation that promoted this Japanization and created, in design as well, a completely Japanese architecture was the aforementioned conception of the hidden roof.

In the hidden roof scheme, a second roof, the exposed roof (*keshōyane*), is installed above the ceiling but beneath the hidden roof. Each of the now three upper space covers—hidden roof structure, exposed or visible roof structure, and ceiling—has its own system of supports, allowing the two roofs to be of different slopes, and the ceiling to be horizontal. From the exterior, one sees only the outer surface of the hidden roof—that is, the roof covering laid over the hidden roof structure—and from the interior one sees only parts of the underside of the exposed roof. The upper portions of the exposed roof and the underside of the hidden roof are always concealed.

The oldest surviving example of the hidden roof construction is found at the Hōryū-ji in the Daikōdō (Main Lecture Hall), which was reconstructed in 990. From the outside the building is entirely a continuation of Tempyō modes of building (pl. 155), but the cross section (pl. 156) clearly shows that a single low ceiling in the main section conceals the roof framework. As a result, the interior space has a quiet, expansive horizontality (pl. 154). In the interior spaces of earlier buildings like the Shin Yakushi-ji main hall (*hondō*; pl. 110) and the Hōryū-ji Dempō-dō (pl. 85), the structural timbers of the undersides of the roof are completely visible, producing an aesthetically powerful effect; at the Tempyō-period Tōshōdai-ji *kondō* (pls. 101, 157) appears the so-called vault of heaven, a high ceiling with intentional monumentality. These effects are lost in the Hōryū-ji Daikōdō, but in their place is a sense of interior space filled with intimate clarity. Because the incline of the exposed rafters over the *hisashi* can be determined independently of the roof, the ceiling could be extended over the entire *moya*, and the rafter ends later came close to being horizontal, eliminating the

183

154.   Daikōdō interior, Hōryū-ji.

previously deep shadow under the eaves. These eaves, along with the corresponding horizontality of the encircling veranda below, give stability and clarity to the exterior appearance, producing an overall tranquility truly Japanese. The interior space is constructed so that even with all the brightness, the dignity of the building is preserved. In the example of the Yakushi-dō of the upper Daigo-ji can be seen, in general, the completion of the change in architectural design due to the hidden roof developed in the Heian period (pl. 158).

    In architecture from the Nara to the Heian periods, there is neither a new bracket system nor a new style of construction. The major evolution, in a word, is toward a Japanese aesthetic of serene curves, and this refinement and stability was made possible by improvements in the hidden roof structure.

155. Daikōdō, Hōryū-ji.

156. Restoration cross section of Daikōdō, Hōryū-ji: 1) strut. 2) tie-beam. 3) rainbow beam. 4) large bearing block. 5) eaves support. 6) flying rafter support. 7) rainbow tie-beam. 8) *hisashi*. 9) ceiling. 10) *moya*. 11) *hisashi*. 12) exposed rafter. 13) flying rafter. 14) hidden rafter. 15) hidden roof. 16) strut. 17) common rafter.

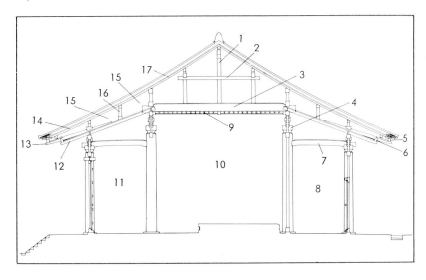

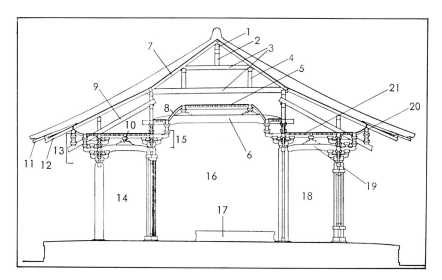

157. Restoration cross section of *kondō*, Tōshōdai-ji: 1) ridge. 2) king post. 3) double transverse beams. 4) strut. 5) ceiling. 6) rainbow beam. 7) common rafter. 8) curved strut (*shirin*). 9) tail rafter. 10) frog-leg strut. 11) flying rafter. 12) base rafter. 13) three-step bracket system. 14) *hisashi*. 15) two-step bracket system. 16) *moya*. 17) Buddhist altar. 18) *hisashi*. 19) rainbow beam. 20) eave purlin. 21) ceiling.

158. Restoration cross section of Yakushi-dō, Daigo-ji: 1) hidden ridge. 2) strut. 3) exposed ridge. 4) hidden roof. 5) strut. 6) transverse beam. 7) strut. 8) brace. 9) eaves support. 10) flying rafter support. 11) frog-leg strut with bearing block. 12) *hisashi*. 13) bracket system parallel to wall plane. 14) strut with bearing block (*kentozuka*). 15) *moya*. 16) ceiling joist. 17) ceiling. 18) one-step bracket system. 19) rainbow tie-beam. 20) *hisashi*. 21) exposed rafter. 22) flying rafter.

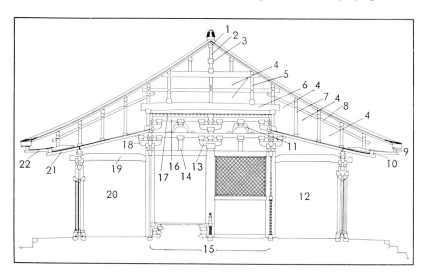

COMBINING THE MAIN HALL AND WORSHIP HALL

The innovations attributable to the hidden roof do not stop at those discussed above, but also include the creation of new space. By the very end of the Heian period, the main hall and worship hall were joined together for the first time at the Taima-dera main hall (Mandara-dō; pl. 159), and the new, deeper main hall became the main current of medieval architecture.

The main hall of Taima-dera was begun during the Nara period. At first it was a simple building with a gable roof, but around the end of the Nara or the beginning of the Heian period, it was changed to a seven-by-four-bay hall by the addition of a one-bay *hisashi* surrounding the original five-by-two-bay inner sanctuary. Along with this change, a worship area was added in the form of a *magobisashi* and over the whole a single roof extended in an uninterrupted line (pl. 160, left). In 1161 the entire structure, except for the inner sanctuary, was demolished and at the same time a worship hall (*raidō*) or outer sanctuary (*gejin*), approximately the same size as the inner sanctuary, was added in front of it. One-bay *hisashi* were built on all four sides, resulting in a seven-by-six-bay hall (pl. 160, right).

In a cross section of the structure (pl. 161) we notice that the ceilings of the inner and outer sanctuaries are installed separately, and above them is the completely unrelated hidden roof structure. It is as if the main hall and worship hall, which heretofore had stood close together with a gutter between them, are now merged under a single large roof. In the past, the front of the main hall, as the formal entrance to a Buddha hall, had pairs of formidable-looking hinged doors, but this was changed here to pairs of latticed sliding doors, allowing the connection between inner and outer sanctuaries to become more intimate (pls. 160, 162). The somewhat dark inner sanctuary could be seen from the outer sanctuary through the transparency of the latticework, and so here was born the medieval style of sometimes combined and other times separate inner and outer sanctuaries.

The deep Buddha hall with a space for worship in the front appears in China by the eleventh century at places like the 1020 Ta-hsiung-pao-tien of Fêng-kuo-ssu at I-hsien, Fêng-t'ien Province, Manchuria. This structure has huge transverse beams placed in front of and behind the line of pillars forming the boundary between the inner and outer sanctuaries, above which several layers of "bottle" struts and transverse beams were piled up, creating a dynamic effect in the structure of the exposed roof framework. The rafters forming a bend at several points create the high roof. Comparing this building with one of native Japanese style, in which one might say the hidden roof is handled separately from the main structure as if to avoid linking directly with the larger framework, the Chinese-style inner space has the structural beauty of upward-thrusting members, along with a consequent power and harshness; the dominant feeling that emerges from the low flat ceiling of the Japanese hall is one of calm and control, and along with the increased depth of the hall there is also an increase in the feeling of seclusion and intimacy.

187

160. Changes in plan of Taima-dera main hall: left, restoration drawing of early Heian-period rebuilding; right, restoration drawing of remodeling about 1161.

159. Main hall, Taima-dera.

It is in the medieval Japanese hall with its hidden roof structure that the native Japanese style comes to its first full fruition. Obvious differences in Chinese and Japanese architectural styles continue from this time, and even the arrival of new Chinese techniques and styles of the Sung dynasty (960–1279) did not deter the continuity of Japanese development. Indeed, at the beginning, the Sung styles were copied closely, but rather than changing the course of the Japanese architectural progression as they had done four hundred years earlier, they were now assimilated and absorbed into a Japanese Buddha hall tradition. The result of the use of the hidden roof structure which appeared at the Taima-dera main hall reveals the culmination of the Japanization of Heian architecture, and at the same time points to the flourishing main hall architecture of the middle ages.

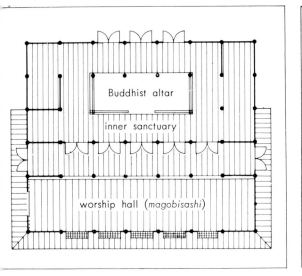

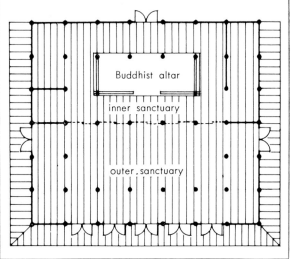

161. Cross section of main hall (Mandara-dō), Taima-dera: 1) hidden roof. 2) ridge. 3) strut. 4) transverse beam. 5) strut with bearing block. 6) frog-leg strut. 7) double rainbow beams with frog-leg struts. 8) rainbow tie-beam. 9) cantilever (*hanegi*). 10) *hisashi*. 11) Buddhist altar. 12) *moya*. 13) inner sanctuary. 14) two-step bracket system. 15) strut. 16) rainbow beam. 17) one-step bracket system. 18) outer sanctuary. 19) *hisashi*. 20) exposed rafter. 21) flying rafter. 22) eaves support. 23) flying rafter support. 24) hidden rafter.

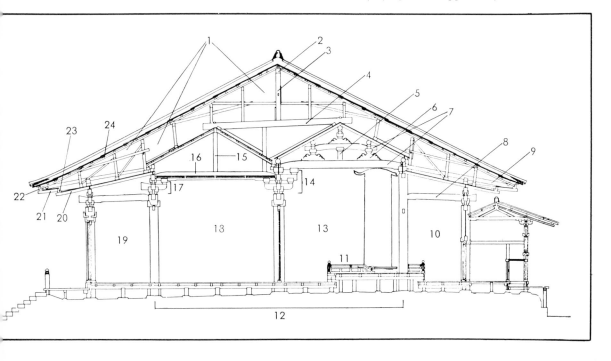

162.   Interior of outer sanctuary, main hall,
Taima-dera.

EARLY BUDDHIST ARCHITECTURE

ARCHITECTURAL DRAWINGS

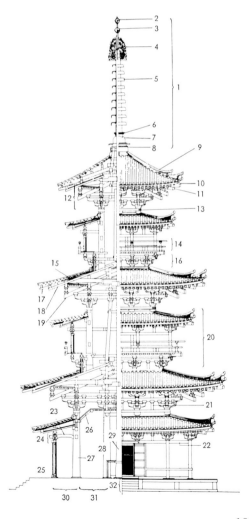

163. Elevation and cross-section drawing of the Yakushi-ji east pagoda: 1) finial (*sōrin*). 2) "sacred jewel" (*hōju*). 3) "dragon wheel" (*ryūsha*). 4) "water flame" (*suien*). 5) "sacred rings" (*hōrin*). 6) "flower bowl" (*ukebana*). 7) "reversed bowl" (*fukubachi*). 8) "dew basin" (*roban*). 9) hip or corner ridge (*sumimune*). 10) flying hip rafter (*hiensumigi*). 11) base hip rafter (*jisumigi*). 12) three-step bracket complex (*mitesaki kumimono*). 13) wall plate (*daiwa*). 14) railing (*kumikōran*). 15) ceiling under eaves (*noki-tenjō*). 16) bracketing under balconies (*koshigumi*). 17) flying rafter (*hiendaruki*). 18) base rafter (*jidaruki*). 19) tail rafter (*odaruki*). 20) *mokoshi*. 21) intercolumnar strut with bearing block (*kentozuka*). 22) head penetrating tie-beam (*kashira-nuki*). 23) rainbow tie-beam (*tsunagi-kōryō*). 24) three-on-one nonprojecting bracket complex (*hira-mitsudo*). 25) *mokoshi* pillar (*mokoshi-bashira*). 26) curved struts (*shirin*). 27) outside or *hisashi* pillars (*gawabashira*). 28) one of four pillars surrounding the altar (*shitenbashira*). 29) central pillar (*shimbashira*). 30) *mokoshi*. 31) *hisashi*. 32) podium (*kidan*).

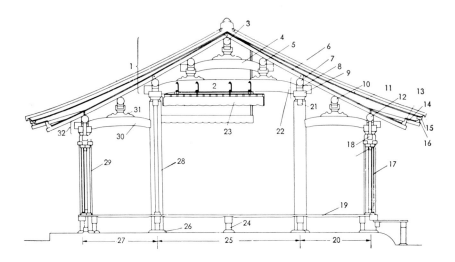

164. Restoration cross-section drawing of Hōryū-ji Dempō-dō: 1) double rainbow beams separated by frog-leg struts (*nijū-kōryō kaerumata shiki kakō*). 2) large rainbow beam (*daikōryō*). 3) ridge pole (*munagi*). 4) upper rainbow beam (*nijū-kōryō*). 5) purlin (*moyageta*). 6) rafter over the *moya* (*moyadaruki*). 7) purlins above the inside (*moya*) pillars (*irigawageta*). 8) bracket arm (*hijiki*). 9) large bearing block (*daito*). 10) purlin (*moyageta*). 11) base rafter (*jidaruki*). 12) eave purlin (*nokigeta*). 13) flying rafter support (*kioi*). 14) flying rafter (*hiendaruki*). 15) eaves filler (*uragō*). 16) eave support (*kayaoi*). 17) plank hinged door (*itatobira*). 18) head penetrating tie-beam (*kashira-nuki*). 19) floorboarding (*yukaita*). 20) *hisashi*. 21) head penetrating tie-beam (*kashira-nuki*). 22) large bearing block with bracket arm (*daito hijiki kumimono*). 23) canopy (*tengai*). 24) floor strut (*yukazuka*). 25) *moya*. 26) base stone (*soseki*). 27) *hisashi*. 28) inside (*moya*) pillars (*irigawabashira*). 29) outside (*hisashi*) pillars (*gawabashira*). 30) rainbow tie-beam (*tsunagi-kōryō*). 31) frog-leg strut (*kaerumata*). 32) large bearing block with bracket arm (*daito hijiki kumimono*).

193

TECHNICAL GUIDE

THE COMPOSITION OF NARA-PERIOD TEMPLES

In the early temple architecture that we see today, including the Hōryū-ji, site of the oldest surviving buildings of Buddhist architecture in Japan, the *kondō* and pagoda alone are usually central to the monastery plan. According to Nara temple records of 747, 263 priests and monks lived at the Hōryū-ji, and 887 at the Daian-ji, and a hustle-and-bustle life flourished among the dormitorylike priests' quarters, which were long narrow buildings divided into many cells. We know that in each cell of the priests' quarters of a Nara temple there were a number of monks living a cooperative life, which had somewhat the character of a research room of graduate students surrounding a professor in the present-day Japanese university. It could well be said that the term "monastery" at that time meant a university of Buddhist studies in which all members lived a collective life. The supporting staff who worked under these priests and were responsible for the daily needs of the priests were also great in number, and the monastic institution was accordingly on a large scale. Related establishments were usually located in one place and titled according to what kind of precinct (*in*) it was. There were certain differences in the name and arrangement at the various temples, but generally they were as described below.

Main Precinct (Butsuden-in)

Arranged in a straight line on the central axis of the monastery were the great south gate, middle gate, *kondō*, and lecture hall, with a semienclosed roofed corridor connecting the middle gate and *kondō*. Left and right of the space between the *kondō* and lecture hall were a belfry and sutra repository, and it was standard for monks' quarters to surround the lecture hall at both sides and in back.

Pagoda Precinct (Tō-in)

The Tempyō monastery plan from the Kōfuku-ji on was arranged with a pagoda precinct separate from that of the main precinct. It is an independent enclosure in which the pagoda stood, surrounded by a semienclosed roofed corridor (*kairō*); the entrance was through a gate, but there were some arrangements which had a corridor across the front on each side of the gate only, and a roofed mud wall surrounding the pagoda precinct on the sides and back. Arrangements in which the pagoda and *kondō* are within the confines of a semienclosed roofed corridor, as have been seen in the Asuka and Hakuhō periods, have combined the main precinct and pagoda precinct.

Refectory and Assembly Precinct (Jikidō and Daishu-in)

The refectory (*jikidō*), kitchen (*ōiya*), and stove rooms (*kamadoya*)—food-stuff and storage rooms attached to the refectory—were arranged in one corner of the monastery, and the administrative offices (*mandokoro*), which regulated the affairs of daily life, were located there

194

also. Although we have some knowledge about the arrangement of this precinct from examples at Kōfuku-ji and Tōdai-ji, many points remain unclear. For instance, the refectory could be either behind or beside the lecture hall, the former seemingly the earlier style. There are also examples which show that when the refectory was at some distance from the side of the lecture hall, a gate and semienclosed roofed corridor were set in front of it. It seems that a facility related to the construction and upkeep of buildings was also placed in the assembly precinct.

Bathhouse Precinct (Onjitsu-in)
One enclosure contained the bathhouse, and since its function gave it a close relationship to the assembly precinct, it should have been placed right beside it or within its area, but the actual arrangement is still not clear.

Storage Precinct (Sōen-in)
The storage precinct was an area in which the temple's storehouses for valuables were placed; the valuables included not only treasured objects but also actual wealth needed to maintain the temple. The highest rank in storage architecture of the time was the *azekura* structure, and several of them were placed in the center of the storage precinct, with both plank and mud storage houses located around them. The storage area was probably surrounded by a strong mud fence. Since the most important storehouses were called *shōsō* ("main storehouses"), this precinct is also known as the *shōsō-in*. The present Shōsō-in in Nara was originally the *shōsō* of Tōdai-ji.

Flower Garden Precinct (Kaen-in)
Place where flowers were grown for presentation before Buddha images and in rituals.

Garden Precinct (En-in)
Thought to be the garden which supplied the vegetable foodstuffs of the monks.

Servants' Precinct (Sen-in)
Place where servants affiliated with the temple lived. The remains of pit-dwellings in the northern sector of the Musashi Kokubun-ji, presumed to have been the servants' quarters, have been discovered. Even at the great temples of the Heijō capital, the majority of the buildings in the assembly precinct and the servants' precinct seem to have been constructed with pillars sunk directly into the ground without the use of stone bases; their roofs were of cypress bark or thatch.

Subsidiary Precinct (Betsu-in)
This precinct is one that had a special purpose and was built in an independent enclosure apart from the above-mentioned fundamental temple composition. Examples are meditation precincts, study and research precincts, and ordination precincts. In addition to the central hall, living quarters were also attached. Thus the monks of the precinct carried out a communal existence more or less separate from that of the main temple. In addition to serving a temporary purpose for Buddhist prayers and austerities, the *betsu-in* could also be a study facility centered around a priest transmitting new doctrines. It could also function as a private prayer hall precinct for certain temple patrons.

195

The Daian-ji (pls. 65, 165) is a good example for showing the sizes and arrangements of the various precincts of such temple complexes. It occupied fifteen square plots (one plot or *chō* was 120 m. by 120 m.), five north to south and three east to west; the Kōfuku-ji and Yakushi-ji were, at one time, about the same size, with the central hall-and-pagoda precinct occupying four plots of the total twelve-plot area. Asuka temples were much smaller. The Asuka-dera and Kawara-dera were probably each only two plots square, and the Hōryū-ji, according to temple records, was about 2.5 plots on each side. A provincial temple (*kokubun-ji*) was supposed to be two plots square, and from excavated remains, many temples seem to have had about these dimensions. The perimeter of the temple grounds was surrounded by a high, roofed daub wall with the great south gate opening at the front (south was generally the main entrance of early Buddhist temples, because of the geomantic orientation to the south, in accordance with continental usage). Gates were also provided at the center of the north, east, and west sides. Sometimes an earthwork was used in place of the covered daub walls at *kokubun-ji* and rural temples.

CHANGES IN THE MONASTERY ARRANGEMENT

Since not nearly enough excavation or investigation of temple sites has been carried out yet, it is quite impossible to make a comparative study of entire temple complexes or even of the most important buildings forming the nuclei. Therefore, when the arrangement of a monastery is mentioned, it is usually only a very few central buildings, such as the *kondō* and pagodas, that are referred to. The existence of a refectory, next in importance to the *kondō* and lecture hall, has been confirmed at no more than two or three temples, and the investigations of priests' quarters have begun to increase only recently. Needless to say, the analysis of the functional aspects of temples as architectural groups is sadly incomplete. Often a monastic arrangement is called by the name of a particular temple which represents that style, and so below, following this custom, I will list the different types, indicating the changes in arrangement in simple terms.

Shitennō-ji Plan

The great south gate, middle gate, pagoda, *kondō*, and lecture hall are arranged on an axis, with a semienclosed roofed corridor connecting the middle gate and lecture hall (pls. 30–31). The pagoda and *kondō* are placed in line with each other within the courtyard of the corridor. In India, at first only the relics of the Buddha were at the center of the Buddhist faith, and then in the course of history followed the appearance of Buddhist images, which in Japan are housed in the *kondō*. Thus the placement of the pagoda in the center of the monastery can be considered the ancient style of monastic arrangement. This is the typical arrangement of Asuka-period monasteries—such as the Shitennō-ji, Wakakusa-dera (the original Hōryū-ji), and Chūgū-ji. At the Asuka-dera the pagoda was surrounded on three sides by Buddha halls, revealing even more clearly that the pagoda was the focal point of the temple (pl. 23).

Kawara-dera Plan

The pagoda and west *kondō* are placed opposite each other to the left and right in the courtyard, on the east-west axis of the south-oriented monastery compound. At the Kawara-dera (pl. 35) and Sūfuku-ji there is a central *kondō* at the center of the north side of the surrounding semienclosed roofed corridor. At the sites of Kanzeon-ji in Tsukushi, near Fukuoka City in Kyushu (pl. 166), and at the Takasaki-dera in Miyagi Prefecture (pl. 167), there was only one *kondō* placed to the west, opposite the pagoda, with the lecture hall at the center of the north side. The temples listed here were official temples, all built around the Tenji era (661–671), except for Takasaki-dera, which was somewhat later. It can be presumed that this style was used mainly on early Hakuhō-period official temples, and that their antiquity succeeds that of the Shitennō-ji style, which seems to have become quickly obsolete. The arrangement of the Yachū-ji, in present-day Habikino City, Osaka Prefecture, built at about the same time, is similar to that of Kanzeon-ji except that the placement of the pagoda and *kondō* was reversed on the east and west axis.

165. Arrangement of Daian-ji monastery (slanted shading for present residental areas, horizontal shading for ponds; compare pl. 65). Numbers in parentheses are keyed below; other numbers are plot numbers (see plate 61): 1) fourth avenue. 2) fifth street. 3) pond and tumulus (covering 1 plot [*chō*], approx. 120 m²). 4) servents' precinct (1½ plots). 5) garden precinct (1 plot). 6) storage precinct (1 plot). 7) flower garden precinct (1 plot). 8) refectory and assembly precinct (1½ plots). 9) main precinct and monks' quarters (4 plots). 10) sixth street. 11) pagoda precinct (4 plots). 12) third avenue.

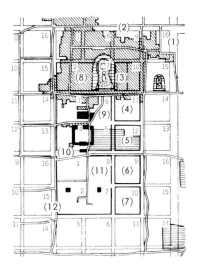

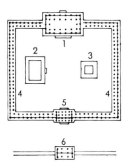

166. Kanzeon-ji monastery plan: 1) lecture hall. 2) pagoda. 3) *kondō*. 4) semienclosed roofed corridor. 5) middle gate. 6) great south gate.

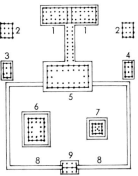

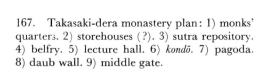

167. Takasaki-dera monastery plan: 1) monks' quarters. 2) storehouses (?). 3) sutra repository. 4) belfry. 5) lecture hall. 6) *kondō*. 7) pagoda. 8) daub wall. 9) middle gate.

197

Hōryū-ji Plan

In contrast to the earlier Kawara-dera style (pl. 35), with pagoda and *kondō* placed facing each other within a courtyard, in the Hōryū-ji plan the fronts of both buildings are arranged facing the direction of the middle gate (pl. 36). At the Hōryū-ji the *kondō* is to the east and the pagoda to the west; when this east-west arrangement is reversed, with the *kondō* on the west and the pagoda on the east, it is called the Hokki-ji plan (there are great doubts, however, as to whether or not the Hokki-ji used the plan to which its name is given). While the plan of the Minami Shiga-dera, in Shiga Prefecture (pl. 168), which is believed to have been an official temple of the Tenji era (661–671), greatly resembles the Kawara-dera arrangement, the small *kondō* on the west and the pagoda on the east are placed facing the middle gate, in the manner of the Hōryū-ji; this would seem to indicate that the Hōryū-ji plan, or the Hokki-ji plan, appeared as an abridged version of the Kawara-dera plan around the time of the Tenji era also. There are also many clan temples of this type. The Koma-dera, Miroku-ji in Gifu Prefecture, Nagakuma-dera ruins, and Ishikawa-dera ruins are all examples of the Hokki-ji plan, and the Yukino-dera and the Sairin-ji should also probably be included in this group. As for the Hōryū-ji plan there are the sites of the Nukada-dera, Ina-dera, Itami-dera (pl. 169), Seinoo-ji, and others. Among these, the Itami-dera and the Seinoo-ji are arranged with the lecture hall aligned centrally behind the *kondō*, and if the central axis of the plan is considered to run through these two buildings, then the pagoda alone is notably out of line to the west; the plans of these two temples have the same character as the later Kōga-dera and the provincial temple (*kokubun-ji*) of Mutsu province (present-day Sendai City, Miyagi Prefecture; pl. 170). The Niihari-dera ruins, in Ibaraki Prefecture, reveal that there was a pagoda on both the east and west sides of the *kondō*.

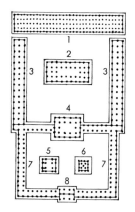

168. Minami Shiga-dera monastery plan: 1) monks' quarters. 2) lecture hall. 3) monks' quarters. 4) *kondō*. 5) small *kondō*. 6) pagoda. 7) semienclosed roofed corridor. 8) middle gate.

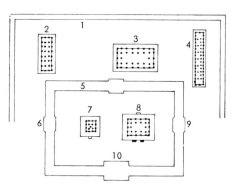

169. Itami-dera monastery plan: 1) roofed mud wall. 2) building at west constructed of pillars embedded in ground without stone bases (monks' quarters?). 3) lecture hall. 4) building at east constructed of pillars embedded in ground without stone bases (monks' quarters?). 5) semi-enclosed roofed corridor. 6) west gate. 7) pagoda. 8) *kondō*. 9) east gate. 10) middle gate.

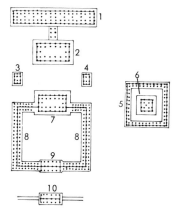

170. Mutsu Kokubun-ji monastery plan: 1) monks' quarters. 2) lecture hall. 3) belfry. 4) sutra repository. 5) semienclosed roofed corridor. 6) pagoda. 7) *kondō*. 8) semienclosed roofed corridor. 9) middle gate. 10) great south gate.

Yakushi-ji Plan

This is a plan with two pagodas, to the left and right in the front courtyard of the *kondō*, the Yakushi-ji of the Fujiwara capital being the representative example. Although two pagodas were built, we can tell from the remains of the central shaft base-stones that Buddha relics were placed in only one of them. There is a reliquary hole in the base stone that once supported the central pillar of the east pagoda at the earlier Yakushi-ji of the Fujiwara capital, and one could be seen in the central pillar base-stone of the west pagoda of the Yakushi-ji at the Heijō capital until reconstruction began a couple of years ago; but there is no place to enshrine relics in either of the companion pagodas. Thus the second pagoda became merely a decorative building with the original meaning lost, apparently built to emphasize the orderly symmetrical arrangement of the monastery. The Kudara-dera of Kawachi province (in present-day Osaka Prefecture) is a similar example (the semienclosed roofed corridors were added to both sides of the *kondō* when it was rebuilt in the Tempyō era [729–749] of Emperor Shōmu's reign; pl. 171). The Tanabe-dera and Takamiya-dera remains in Osaka are among numerous examples there of temples with the twin pagoda style. The Miroku-ji at Usa, in Ōita Prefecture, Kyushu, built between 739 and 743, was also of the Yakushi-ji plan. This temple was built with the intention of deepening the ties between the imperial court and the Usa Hachiman Shrine. The sphere of influence of the Yakushi-ji plan was limited to the Kinai area (Nara, Osaka, and parts of Kyoto and Hyōgo Prefectures) and such special areas as Usa, and it seems to have been of comparatively short duration, being limited to only the early Tempyō period.

199

171. Kawachi Kudara-dera monastery plan:
1) refectory. 2) lecture hall. 3) *kondō* remains.
4) west pagoda remains. 5) east pagoda remains.
6) middle gate remains. 7) south gate remains.
8) daub wall. 9) east precinct (?).

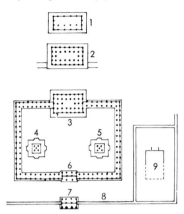

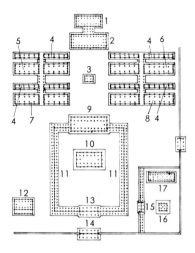

Kōfuku-ji Plan

A style in which the pagoda is moved away from the central monastery compound, it is first seen at Kōfuku-ji built within the Heijō capital (pl. 64). The great south gate, middle gate, *kondō*, and lecture hall are arranged in a straight line to the north in the center of the monastery, and the pagoda is placed in a separate precinct. The courtyard, which was surrounded by a semienclosed roofed corridor and entered from the middle gate, was probably the location of ceremonies performed before the *kondō*; the Buddha images in the *kondō* are believed to have been the center of the monastery's devotions. The original role of the pagoda as the repository of a holy relic at the time Buddhism entered Japan became less important thereafter; and by the time of the popularity of the Kōfuku-ji plan it had come to function as monastery scenery. At the Gangō-ji (pl. 172), where the pagoda was built in a similar separate precinct, the surrounding semienclosed roofed corridor extends to the lecture hall, and the *kondō* is an independent building inside the courtyard. This plan retains vestiges of the monasteries of the Asuka and Hakuhō periods, but it had no imitators. From the Tempyō period onward we come to an architectural phase in which the Kōfuku-ji plan, with semienclosed roofed corridor attached to both sides of the *kondō*, flourished, and there are many examples of it among provincial temples (*kokubun-ji*). There is generally a single pagoda, but among the many establishments which had two pagodas are the Daian-ji, Tōdai-ji, Saidai-ji, Hokke-ji, and Akishino-dera, all official temples of the Heijō capital. Those which have pagodas placed east and west midway between the great south gate and middle gate are classified as the Tōdai-ji style, and those with pagodas placed outside and in front of the great south gate are said to be in the Daian-ji style.

Important Architectural Features of the Monastery

Gates and Semienclosed Roofed Corridors (Mon and Kairō)

There are two kinds of gates—one, like the great south gate, that is in the outer wall and

200

172. Gangō-ji monastery plan: 1) mess hall (*ji-kiden*). 2) refectory (*jikidō*). 3) belfry. 4) acolytes' quarters. 5) northwestern monks' quarters. 6) Higashi-muro, northern monks' quarters. 7) southwestern monks' quarters. 8) Higashi-muro, southern monks' quarters. 9) lecture hall. 10) *kondō*. 11) semienclosed roofed corridor. 12) hall housing miniature pagodas. 13) middle gate. 14) great south gate. 15) middle gate. 16) pagoda. 17) monks' quarters. 18) east gate.

173. Interior of great east gate, Hōryū-ji.

opens on a roofed daub fence which surrounds the perimeter of the temple grounds; the other, the middle gate, which is inside the compound and some distance from the great south gate and which, with the semienclosed roofed corridors attached on each side, protects the main precinct and pagoda precinct at the front. Surviving examples of gates in the outer wall from the ancient period are the great east gate of Hōryū-ji (pl. 173) and the Tegai Gate (the north gate on the west side of the Tōdai-ji), and in the inner precinct the middle gate and surrounding semienclosed roofed corridor of the Hōryū-ji. The two former structures, representative examples of Tempyō-period outer gates, are three-by-two-bay "eight-legged gates" (four main pillars down the center and eight secondary pillars) with a center-bay entrance. There are no great south gates from this ancient period,* but judging from the sites of Asuka-dera and Kawara-dera, eight-legged gates of these same styles seem to have been built there. As time passed the great south gate came to be a two-storied gate of five bays across and three portals, examples of which are known at the Kōfuku-ji, Daian-ji, Yaku-shi-ji, and Tōdai-ji. The Suzaku Gate of the Heijō capital, which corresponds exactly to the dimensions of the Daian-ji great south gate, is shown in a scale model reconstruction in plate 174, and it is believed that the Daian-ji gate was of about the same style. The Hōryū-ji middle gate is a two-storied gate, four bays across by three bays deep. The Asuka-dera middle gate was also much larger than the great south gate, being three bays longer in both directions and presumed to have had two stories. In contrast to these, the Daian-ji and Yakushi-ji middle gates were five bays across, about the same size as the great south gate, but the dimensions of their depth became smaller, and they seem to have had only a single story with gabled roofs. During the Asuka and early Hakuhō periods the combination of a single-story great south gate and two-storied middle gate is thought to have been common, but in the Tempyō period there was a sudden reversal; the great south gate became two storied while the middle gate became a single-storied structure.

* The present great south gate of Tōdai-ji was built during the Kamakura period, in 1199, on the foundations of the 1161 reconstruction.

174. Restoration model of Suzaku Gate, Heijō palace. (Nara National Research Institute of Cultural Properties)

There were both single- and double-aisled semienclosed roofed corridors. The Asuka-dera, Kawara-dera, Hōryū-ji, and other temples had single corridors, but later the first-class temples in the Heijō capital had double ones. Furthermore, in the east precinct of Hōryū-ji, the Yumedono (which corresponds to the *kondō*) and the lecture hall (Dempō-dō) are buildings with podia and tile roofs, but they are enclosed by semienclosed roofed corridors with middle gates which all have pillars sunk directly in the ground without the use of base stones and are covered by cypress-bark roofs.

Pagodas (Tō or Tōba)

The pagodas which are extant from the Nara period are the Hōryū-ji west precinct five-story pagoda (the first story has a *mokoshi*), the Hokki-ji three-story pagoda, the Yakushi-ji east pagoda (three stories, each with a *mokoshi*), and the Taima-dera three-story east pagoda, plus the five-story miniature pagodas of the Kairyūō-ji and the Gangō-ji Gokuraku-bō. In each case the first story is three bays square, but the huge nine-story pagoda at Daikandai-ji and a number of pagodas elsewhere (none of which are extant) were five bays square on the first story. There are no particular structural differences between pagodas of three and five stories. In each case, four pillars are erected inside the first story and surround a central pillar that extends up from its base to the *sōrin*, the bronze finial seen on the top of the pagoda. This central pillar differs with the era. In Asuka-period pagodas, like those at the Asuka-dera, Shitennō-ji, or Chūgū-ji, the base stone for the central pillar is set about three meters down from the top surface of the podium, and is firmly embedded in the hard packed earth. The Hōryū-ji and Hōrin-ji are also examples with this type of central pillar base stone. Central pillar base stones of the Hakuhō period—for example, those of Kawara-dera, Sūfuku-ji, and Koma-dera—were more shallowly set, being placed only about one meter down from the surface of the podium. From the Yakushi-ji of the Fujiwara capital on, the central pillar base stone is installed on top of the podium in the same way as other foundation stones. This is related to the method of digging deeply and packing the earth when the foundation was made, and in the Asuka period the central pillar base stone was placed on the very bottom and is therefore the deepest set.

In addition to the Asuka-dera, Shitennō-ji, and the Hōryū-ji, which are examples of arrangements where Buddhist relics are placed in holes hollowed out from the top surface of the central pillar base stone, at Sūfuku-ji and Koma-dera holes for relics are cut into the sides of the central pillar base stones. Yet there are many central pillar base stones which have no reliquary chambers in them, so it seems that the reliquary space was not uniformly made. The reliquary hole was simply made in Asuka times, but during the Hakuhō period a shallow circular space was dug out of the base stone into which the central pillar was placed, and a reliquary hole was made in the center of this space. It seems that semicircular wooden braces were placed flush on three or four sides of the central pillar to give it added support; the Hōryū-ji five-story pagoda provides an example of this. The circular holes cut in the central pillar base stones at the Tachibana-dera and Wakakusa-dera sites have small semicircular holes around the circumference to accommodate these braces. In the Tempyō period a tenon was placed at the center of the base stone to fit into the mortise on the bottom of the central pillar. This became the general style. Thus the central pillar base stone was no longer used for enshrining Buddhist relics. At the west pagoda of Taima-dera the relics were installed at the top of the central pillar, and there must have been many other examples of this placement.

Beyond the second story of the pagoda there is no interior equipment or flooring, so that it is ordinarily impossible for any but repairman to ascend. A Buddha altar is placed within the four main pillars on the first story, but at the Hōryū-ji five-story pagoda groups of clay images illustrating Buddhist legends are enshrined. There were eight images of Śākyamuni in the Yakushi-ji east and west pagodas (pl. 175). The octagonal eight-story pagoda planned

175. Interior of east pagoda, Yakushi-ji.

203

at the Saidai-ji ended in failure, but the site of an octagonal pagoda from the ruins of the Katagihara-dera have been discovered. Thus the octagonal nine-story pagoda of the Hōshō-ji, dating from the Heian period (1083), was not the first. We know that eight-sided multistoried pagodas were built from the early Nara period on.

Kondō

Kondō extant from the ancient period are those of Hōryū-ji and Tōshōdai-ji. In the Asuka and Hakuhō periods *kondō* were independent buildings which stood in proximity to the pagoda, within the courtyard surrounded by the semienclosed roofed corridors; for this reason, *kondō* plans were usually nearly square, being five by four bays, with two stories, so that the buildings gave a balanced appearance from all sides. The Hōryū-ji *kondō* is of this standard type, and the middle *kondō* of the Asuka-dera was also about the same. The *moya*, the central three-by-two-bay core, was the place to enshrine Buddha images. At present, the Hōryū-ji *kondō* has a white plastered earthen platform in its *moya*, but originally a simple Buddha altar was made by running nonpenetrating tie-beams (*nageshi*) a short distance from the floor around the *moya* pillars and laying planks on top of them. At large temples from the Yakushi-ji on, the scale of the *kondō* was increased to seven bays across and four bays in depth. As in the previous period, they were two-storied structures, and at Yakushi-ji in particular, the pagoda and *kondō* were of a similar style in the placement of a *mokoshi* on each story (pl. 176). However, when the semienclosed roofed corridor was attached to both sides of the *kondō*, as at Kōfuku-ji, only the appearance from the front was considered important, and the *kondō* was made a high single-storied building with its main frame seven-by-four bays. Around this perimeter, wide *mokoshi* were attached, giving it the appearance, from the exterior, of a two-storied building. The original Tōdai-ji Great Buddha Hall (Daibutsu-den) was also of the same style (pl. 177), and one advantage was the increased height of the interior space. When there are actually two stories, the upper story is completely ornamental, like the upper stories of a pagoda, and a rather low ceiling was installed on the first-story interior. Such structural changes in the Tempyō period are probably related to the enshrining of monumental Buddha images. The roofs of the independent *kondō* of the Asuka and Hakuhō periods were hip-and-gable; but the Kōfuku-ji and Tōdai-ji *kondō* are assumed to have been hipped-roof buildings; in contrast to the former, which stand severely alone, the latter have a harmonious spread left and right, connecting to the roofed corridors on both sides.

Since the Tōshōdai-ji was a second-class temple, the *kondō* was limited to one story, and had a hipped roof. But when we look at the measurements, we find that the central bay was sixteen Tempyō *shaku* (one *shaku* equals about thirty centimeters) and the ones to its immediate right and left were fifteen *shaku*, then thirteen *shaku*, and the two end bays were eleven *shaku*, so that the successive diminution in width is obvious. We can see from this that the frontal aspect of this building, which was connected to the roofed corridor, was given considerable attention. Compared to this, at the Kawara-dera and the Yakushi-ji *kondō* (first-class temples), the horizontal measurements of the *moya* bays were all the same, and the bay lengths of the *hisashi* on both ends were only slightly narrower. The one-bay open porch along the front of the Tōshōdai-ji *kondō* is another special feature of the Tempyō period; it is treated as an extension of the semienclosed roofed corridor that surrounds the courtyard, and the idea appears to have been to incorporate the whole of the courtyard into the *kondō* in a more intimate manner.

Aside from the *kondō* mentioned above is the west *kondō* of Kairyūō-ji, and among the Buddha halls of subsidiary precincts (*betsu-in*) are the Hokke-dō of Tōdai-ji and the main hall of the Shin Yakushi-ji; also included are the Hōryū-ji Yumedono and the Eizan-ji Hakkaku-dō, which are both octagonal Buddha halls.

176. Restoration model of *kondō*, Yakushi-ji.

177. Restoration model of Daibutsu-den, Tōdai-ji. (Tōdai-ji)

Lecture Halls and Refectories (Kōdō and Jikidō)

Both the lecture hall and the refectory were buildings on a large scale in order to hold a gathering of all the monks of a monastery. In monasteries of the Asuka and Hakuhō periods, especially, when the *kondō* was not so large, the lecture hall was the largest building of the temple complex. However, the construction of these utilitarian buildings was simple, and all were single storied except for the Yakushi-ji lecture hall, which had a *mokoshi*. Lecture halls extant from the Nara period are the Hōryū-ji east precinct Dempō-dō and the Tōshōdai-ji lecture hall, and although the main lecture hall (Daikōdō) of the west precinct of Hōryū-ji was reconstructed in the Heian period, it well preserves the form of the earlier period. The former two structures were palace buildings converted into lecture halls, seven and nine bays in length, respectively, and both four bays deep, with simple support systems of large bearing blocks plus bracket arms (*daito-hijiki*). The reason why the Dempō-dō has a gabled roof and plank floor is because it followed its former residential form; as a lecture hall, it should, according to principle, have an earthen floor and a hip-and-gable or hipped roof, like the lecture hall of the Tōshōdai-ji. Though a large building, it has bracket complexes with simple large bearing blocks and bracket arms (*daito-hijiki*); this is probably due to its following the standard for lecture halls of second-rank temples. The Hōryū-ji west precinct lecture hall (Daikōdō) is now nine bays across (originally it was only eight), and uses a three block on one bracket arm system (*mitsudo-gumi*). It can be presumed from the Asuka-dera site that the lecture hall was eight bays across, much larger than the *kondō* and all the other buildings in the monastery. The lecture hall of the Kōfuku-ji, a first-rank temple of the Tempyō period, was nine bays by four, and by the time of the building of the Tōdai-ji lecture hall was enlarged to eleven bays across. The inside of the lecture hall was a large earthen-floor room, with only a rather small Buddha altar built in the center. Standard practice called for raised seats for high-ranking priests, called "discussion platforms," to be placed to the left and right in front of the altar, and during such Buddhist ceremonies as those focusing on the Vimalakīrti Sutra or the Lotus Sutra, the monks would sit, with legs drawn up, on benches lined up on the earthern floor and listen to discussions of the religious texts.

No Nara-period refectory still stands, and there are few confirmed examples of remains. The Hōryū-ji refectory was originally an administrative office (*mandokoro*) of three interior rooms, but it was converted into a refectory in the Heian period. At that time a narrow hall (*hosodono*) was added in front, and the outer walls of the main structure and narrow hall were joined together, forming twin halls (*narabidō*), and the interior was remodeled to function as one deep room. Thus the need for a wide earthern floor in the refectory was satisfied by combining the buildings. The Kōfuku-ji refectory was also a large-scale nine-by-five-bay building, which later had a nine-by-two *hosodono* built in front. From documents we know the Yakushi-ji, Gangō-ji, and Tōdai-ji refectories to have been large buildings of eleven bays across. In the refectory interior there were only images of holy monks, and it was the place where the monks sat, with legs drawn up on mats placed on the benches arranged on the earthen floor, and ate according to a prescribed manner. This practice has been handed down even today at Tōdai-ji's Nigatsu-dō, where it is followed during the ceremony known at the Shū'ni-e.

Belfries and Sutra Repositories (Shurō and Kyōzō)

These two buildings were commonly built in front of the lecture hall, to the east and west, although it has recently become clear that, at the Yakushi-ji, they were placed to the east and west between the lecture hall and refectory. At Hōryū-ji's west precinct, only the sutra repository remains of the pair from the Nara period. The first belfry that stood opposite it was destroyed in a fire, and later, in about 990 of the Heian period, it was rebuilt (pl. 178) along with the main lecture hall (Daikōdō). Both belfry and sutra repository are three-by-two-bay two-story structures with earthen floors on the first stories and plank floors and surrounding verandas on the second stories. Inside, the ascent to the upper floor is made by means of a ladder. Under the veranda both buildings use bracket complexes consisting of bracket arms set at right angles and each carrying three small bearing blocks, and the upper story has double rainbow-beams with frog-leg struts together with bracket arms on which are set three bearing blocks placed in the direction of the wall plane. The two buildings at first seem quite similar, but when one looks closely one notices that the lower story of the sutra repository is tall and the upper story has a light appearance, whereas the height of the upper story of the belfry has been increased; and since the roof has a rather sharp incline, the upper story seems heavy. The light appearance of the former style is lost. Yet these differences derive from the periods in which the buildings were constructed, and while we may say that the buildings are almost identical, the Heian structure is lacking in a certain elegance. In the upper story of the belfry is hung a large bell.

Obviously, all the sutras of the temple could not be stored in a building the size of the sutra repository; actually, they were stored in a log storehouse or a storehouse of some other type. But more than a utility building, the sutra repository was important in regulating the daily life of the monks; the sutra repository and belfry symbolized the significance of revering the sutras and proclaiming the hour. In later Zen monasteries a drum tower was built as well.

178. Belfry, west precinct, Hōryū-ji.

The belfry and sutra repository of a Nara-period monastery were of the two-storied style, whose standard size seems to have been three bays by two. In belfries of the Heian period, walls which broaden at the base, like a flared skirt (*hakama-goshi*), were used on the lower story. The Hōryū-ji east precinct belfry (pl. 179), built in the Heian period, is the oldest example of this style, but the materials of its present state are mostly replacements, the building having undergone extensive repairs during the Kamakura period.

Monks' Quarters (Sōbō)

Monks' dormitories were long, narrow, gable-roofed buildings partitioned into individual cells. One cell, two or three bays wide, was completely cut off from the cells on either side by walls. Since the buildings were built with six to nine cells, the dormitories could extend from over ten to more than twenty bays long. Dormitories were located near the lecture hall, often on both sides and behind. The arrangement on three sides of the lecture hall was used at Kawara-dera, Kōfuku-ji, and Tōdai-ji, but at Yakushi-ji the dormitories were placed on either side of the refectory, at the northeast and northwest corners. At the Gangō-ji, the dormitories were lined up horizontally, parallel to each other, running only east and west. At Tōshōdai-ji, dormitories oriented north-south were built to the east and west of the lecture hall. In any case, there was never a definite arrangement. At provincial temples (*kokubun-ji*), there are also examples of dormitories being placed behind the lecture hall, running east-west, in which a central space of five bays wide was given over to a refectory and, to the east and west of this, five cells of two-bay width each provided for the monks' living quarters.

Since dormitories were the most utilized buildings, none remains from the Nara period, but the Hōryū-ji Higashi-muro (East Dormitory) and the Gangō-ji Gokuraku-bō Zenshitsu (pl. 180) not only adhere to the plan and scale of that period, but old materials were re-used in building them, so that we know from them what Nara-period monks' residences looked like. Moreover, the two cells at the northern end of the Higashi-muro have been restored to their original form.

The Hōryū-ji Nishi-muro (West Dormitory) and the Tōshōdai-ji Higashi-muro were built in the Kamakura period, but adhere closely to the Nara-period monks' residence style. Originally, Hōryū-ji's Higashi-muro had eight cells totaling about fifty meters in length, but at present the southern half has been converted to the Shōryō-in, and only the four cells in the northern half now remain. The present exterior appearance is the result of extensive remodeling in the Muromachi period (1392–1572), but the line of alternating doors and vertically slatted windows hands down a trace of the ancient period when one cell was two bays wide. In the two cells restored to their original form (each two bays by four bays), the center core (*moya*) is two bays deep by two bays wide and was a sleeping chamber; the front *hisashi* was an anteroom, and the back *hisashi* was divided into an entranceway and a one-bay-square private room.

The organization is about the same in the case of a three-bay cell. At the Gangō-ji priests' quarters (pl. 181), private rooms in the rear were made on both sides, and consequently from the outside a three-bay-wide area with a hinged door and vertically slatted windows on each side indicates a one-cell unit. Unlike the much simpler Hōryū-ji Higashi-muro, which does not employ bracketing (the purlins being placed directly atop the pillars), the Gangō-ji priest's

179. Belfry, east precinct, Hōryū-ji.

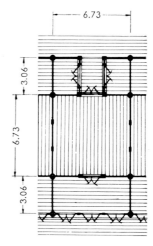

181. Restoration drawing of cell in monks' dormitory, Gangō-ji (measurements in meters).

180. Zenshitsu, Gokuraku-bō, Gangō-ji.

quarters use nonprojecting brackets with three bearing blocks, and the eaves are also double those of the Hōryū-ji Higashi-muro; this was presumably the standard style for priests' dormitories of first-rank temples. From the earthen floors at the Tōdai-ji and the Hōryū-ji we know that chairs were used. Gangō-ji had a plank floor, but because the slatted windows are placed high, it suggests the custom of using chairs. In addition to the above-mentioned large cells for priests there were also small cells for lower-ranking monks. In contrast to the upper-rank priests' cells, which were usually four bays deep (approximately ten to twelve meters), the lower-ranking monks' cells were only about two bays deep (about four to five meters), built behind and in line with the larger buildings. The large and small dormitories were used as a pair. Aside from both buildings being compartmentalized into cell units of the same length, the inner garden was also partitioned off by erecting fences on the boundaries of each cell. From the additional information found in temple records, it seems probable that anywhere from five to nine priests lived in one cell—the head priests occupying the larger cells, their followers living in the shallower cells. In total area each person would occupy an area of nine square meters, but since part of this area would be anterooms and passageways, each person actually had only about six square meters of living space. While dating from the Heian period, the Tsuma-muro at Hōryū-ji is the sole survivor among the dormitories for lower-ranking monks (pl. 182).

182. Tsuma-muro (right) and Higashi-muro (left), Hōryū-ji.

Storage Spaces (Kura)

The storehouse regarded as the very best was the log type (*azekura*) with a raised floor, of which a fair number remain. At Tōdai-ji, beginning with the Shōsō-in treasure repository there are the Hombō sutra repository, Tamukeyama Shrine treasure repository, Hokke-dō sutra repository, and the Kanjinsho sutra repository, and at Tōshōdai-ji there are the treasure and sutra repositories—all in the *azekura* style. With the exception of the Tōdai-ji Shōsō-in, the other four Tōdai-ji buildings were moved from other places within the temple compound in recent times, and the last two seem to come from the Heian period. The Tō-ji (Kyōō-gokoku-ji) treasure repository is also an *azekura* building of the Heian period.

Structurally, all *azekura* buildings are much the same, with floors raised off the ground and floor-plates (*daiwa*) constructed on the floor posts, above which are walls composed of logs whose ends overlap as in a log cabin. In cross section, the logs are five sided with flat backs, which makes the storehouse exterior walls corrugated and those of the interior flat. Two or three of the uppermost logs are lengthened so that they extend outward at the corners to receive the eave purlins. The extant roofs are all hipped, but originally the Tōshōdai-ji sutra repository had a gabled roof; from this, we know that, even with *azekura* buildings, the simple ones were made with a gable roof. There were twin as well as single storehouses, and the Shōsō-in is an example of the twin type (*narabi-kura*). The two storehouses of the Shōsō-in were joined by enclosing the middle space with planks, creating an additional storage area. All three sections were covered by one hipped roof, and each storage chamber opens with a hinged plank door on the front. The style has also been called *mitsugura* ("triple storehouse").

The Hōryū-ji Kōfū-zō is not in the *azekura* style, but it does express an early stage of the twin storage hall form. Judging from the technical detail, the building appears to be early Heian. While it is in the raised-floor style with floor supports on which floor-plates are placed, above the floor-plates stand square pillars, and walls of mud and plaster. Behind the walls thick planks are extended between the square pillars, with the result that the walls are considerably more solid than they look from the outside. Of the nine-bay-long building, only the three bays on each end were made into storehouses, while the central three bays are open and lack floor planks; the entryways to the north and south storehouses face each other and open toward the central space. When a door was opened, it seems that floor-boards were placed temporarily over the floor joists in the central space. The reason why the doors were placed as described is because if they were placed on the outer walls, they would be exposed directly to wind and rain. This arrangement, therefore, resulted from a careful consideration of the important treasures that were moved in and out. The twin storehouse originally had this shape. From early drawings we know that the Kōfuku-ji storehouse (*shōsō*) was also made in this style, using *azekura* structure.

211

LIST OF EXTANT STRUCTURES

ASUKA AND NARA PERIODS

Buddha Halls: Hōryū-ji *kondō*, Kairyūō-ji west *kondō*, Tōdai-ji Hokke-dō, Tōshōdai-ji *kondō*, Shin Yakushi-ji main hall

Octagonal Halls: Hōryū-ji east precinct Yumedono, Eizan-ji octagonal hall

Pagodas: Hōryū-ji five-story pagoda, Hokki-ji three-story pagoda; Yakushi-ji east pagoda, Kairyūō-ji five-story miniature pagoda, Gangō-ji Gokuraku-bō five-story miniature pagoda, Taima-dera east pagoda

Lecture Halls: Tōshōdai-ji lecture hall, Hōryū-ji east precinct Dempō-dō

Gates: Hōryū-ji middle gate, Hōryū-ji great east gate, Tōdai-ji Tegai Gate

Semienclosed Roofed Corridors and Others: Hōryū-ji semienclosed roofed corridors (2), Hōryū-ji sutra repository, Hōryū-ji Higashi-muro, Hōryū-ji refectory

HEIAN PERIOD

Buildings at Nara-Period Temples: Hōryū-ji Daikōdō, Hōryū-ji west precinct belfry, Hōryū-ji Kōfū-zō, Hōryū-ji Tsuma-muro, Taima-dera west pagoda, Taima-dera Mandara-dō, Tōdai-ji Hokke-dō sutra repository, Tōdai-ji Kanjinsho sutra repository, Kyōōgokoku-ji (Tō-ji) treasure hall, Kōryū-ji lecture hall

Buildings at Mountain Temples or Esoteric Monasteries: Murō-ji five-story pagoda, Murō-ji *kondō*, Daigo-ji five-story pagoda, Daigo-ji Yakushi-dō, Ishiyama-dera main hall, Ichijō-ji three-story pagoda, Kakurin-ji Taishi-dō

Buildings at Pure Land Monasteries: Byōdō-in Hōō-dō (four buildings: middle hall, two wings, and back corridor), Jōruri-ji main hall, Jōruri-ji three-story pagoda, Sanzen-in main hall, Chūson-ji Konjiki-dō, Kōzō-ji Amida hall, Fuki-dera Daidō

Miscellaneous—Sambutsu-ji Nageire-dō

A note on the above list: The date of the Murō-ji five-story pagoda falls on the borderline between the Nara and Heian periods; although it is often included in the Nara period, my classification assigns it to the Heian period. Further, I have not listed structures such as the Daigo-ji *kondō*, the Kongō-ji "many treasures" pagoda (*tahōtō*) in Osaka Prefecture, and the Chūson-ji sutra repository, which, although erected in the Heian period, were extensively repaired in later periods. In addition, the Hokke-dō sutra repository and Kanjinsho sutra repository at Tōdai-ji, which are usually thought of as belonging to the Nara period, have been classified as Heian-period structures; and the Hōkai-ji Amida hall (in Kyoto), the Kakurin-ji Jōgyō-dō, and the Getsurin-ji Yakushi-dō (Yamaguchi Pref.), the Daihō-ji main hall (Ehime Pref.), the Buraku-ji Yakushi-dō (Kōchi Pref.), and others, which have been counted among structures surviving from the Heian period, are here considered to be of the Kamakura period and have thus been excluded from the list.

Chūson-ji—Hiraizumi, Hiraizumi-chō, Nishi Iwai-gun, Iwate-ken.

Kōzō-ji—Takakura, Kakuda-shi, Miyagi-ken.

Ganjō-ji—Shiramizu-machi, Uchigō, Iwaki-shi, Fukushima-ken.

Ishiyama-dera—Terabe-machi, Ishiyama, Ōtsu-shi, Shiga-ken.

Kōryū-ji—Hachigaoka-chō, Uzumasa, Ukyō-ku, Kyōto-shi, Kyōto-fu.

Sanzen-in—Raigōin-chō, Ōhara, Sakyō-ku, Kyōto-shi, Kyōto-fu.

Daigo-ji—Garan-chō, Daigo, Fushimi-ku, Kyōto-shi, Kyōto-fu.

Kyōōgokoku-ji (Tō-ji)—Kujō-chō, Minami-ku, Kyōto-shi, Kyōto-fu.

Byōdō-in—Ujirenge, Uji-shi, Kyōto-fu.

Jōruri-ji—Ōaza Nishio, Kamo-chō, Sōraku-gun, Kyōto-fu.

Kakurin-ji—Kakogawa-chō, Kakogawa-shi, Hyōgo-ken.

Ichijō-ji—Sakamoto, Hōjō, Kasai-shi, Hyōgo-ken.

Tōdai-ji—Zōshi-chō, Nara-shi, Nara-ken.

Shin Yakushi-ji—Takabatake-chō, Nara-shi, Nara-ken.

Gangō-ji Gokuraku-bō—Nakain-chō, Nara-shi, Nara-ken.

Yakushi-ji—Nishi-no-kyō-machi, Nara-shi, Nara-ken.

Tōshōdai-ji—Gojō-chō, Nara-shi, Nara-ken.

Kairyūō-ji—Hokkeji-chō, Nara-shi, Nara-ken.

Eizan-ji—Kotori-chō, Gojō-shi, Nara-ken.

Taima-dera—Ōaza Taima, Taima-chō, Kita Katsuragi-gun, Nara-ken.

Hōryū-ji—Ōaza Hōryūji, Ikaruga-chō, Ikoma-gun, Nara-ken.

Hokki-ji—Ōaza Okamoto, Ikaruga-chō, Ikoma-gun, Nara-ken.

Murō-ji—Ōaza Murō, Murō-mura, Uda-gun, Nara-ken.

Sambutsu-ji—Mitoku, Misasa-chō, Tōhaku-gun, Tottori-ken.

Fuki-dera—Ōaza Fuki, Bungo Takada-shi, Ōita-ken.

LIST OF ILLUSTRATIONS IN JAPANESE

GLOSSARY

amidadō (阿弥陀堂; Amida hall): the most important and popular hall of the Pure Land Buddhist temple complex beginning in the mid-Heian period. It is dedicated to Amida (Amitābha), the Buddha of the Western Paradise. See plates 148–49, 151–53.

Amida hall. See *amidadō*.

Asuka period (593–661): period of Japanese history named after the village of Asuka in the Yamato plain. Two of the most influential ruler-patrons of the period were the empress Suiko (r. 592–628) and her nephew and regent, Prince Shōtoku, during whose lifetimes the Asuka-dera and the Shitennō-ji, among other monasteries, were built.

azekura-zukuri (校倉造): the architectural style of storehouses built out of logs, especially popular in the Nara period (662–781). The Tōdai-ji Shōsō-in is its most representative example. See plate 93.

bay. See *ken*.

belfry. See *shurō*.

boat-shaped bracket arm. See *funa-hijiki*.

bracket arm. See *hijiki*.

bracket system. See *tokyō*.

Buddha hall. See *butsuden*.

butsuden (仏殿; Buddha hall): In the ancient period a general term for all structures that housed one or more images of Buddhas, bodhisattvas, and/or other figures; also called *butsudō* (仏堂) and *bukkaku* (仏閣). A *butsuden* is not necessarily the main hall of a monastery.

chūmon (中門; middle gate): the inner gate of the monastery. In the earliest establishments it was always located in the center front, on the same axis as the great south gate, and joined the semienclosed roofed corridor on its left and right sides. See plates 36, 40.

daito. See *masu*.

frog-leg struts. See *kaerumata*.

Fujiwara no Michinaga (966–1027): Fifth son of Fujiwara no Kaneie, Michinaga brought the Fujiwara family to the zenith of its power through imperial marriage and intrigue, eventually placing a grandson, and then a son on the throne. Having secured the position of his descendents, he became a monk affiliated with Tōdai-ji in 1018, and in 1020 began the building of the Hōjō-ji on his own domain.

Fujiwara period (898–1184): the late Heian period, time of the supremacy of the aristocratic Fujiwara family and of their patronage of a more elaborate, decorative style in the arts, which contrasted sharply with the austerity of Esoteric monuments of a century before. In architecture the major extant monuments of the Fujiwara period are the Byōdō-in and Chūson-ji.

funa-hijiki (舟肘木; "boat-shaped" bracket arm): the simplest and probably earliest form of the bracket arm, possibly pre-Buddhist. It was flat on the top and curved on the bottom, and was often set within the wall plane, not projecting from it. Used in simple Japanese structures even today, its origins are probably Chinese, and it can be seen at the fifth-century Tun-huang caves. See plate 17.

gabled roof construction. See *kirizuma-zukuri*.

godaidō (五大堂; "hall of the Five Radiant Kings"): a type of Esoteric Buddhist hall popular from the mid-Heian period on, dedicated to the Godai Myō-ō, deities who manifest the righteous wrath of the Buddhist pantheon. This hall is often found to the east of the *kondō* when an Amida hall is built to the west.

great south gate. See *nandaimon*.

Hakuhō period (662–710): name for the

early Nara period, which comprised the reigns of seven emperors and four empresses, including Emperor Temmu and the empresses Gemmei and Jitō. The representative monument of the period is Hōryū-ji, but other monastery building projects, like the Hōrin-ji and Hokki-ji, were also carried out in the Nara region.

Heian period (782–1184): This long period of Japanese history is named after its capital city of Heian, part of present-day Kyoto. Architecturally the early Heian period is represented by the introduction of Esoteric monastic styles of the Shingon and Tendai sects, the most famous temples being the Enryaku-ji on Mount Hiei, the Kongōbu-ji on Mount Kōya, the Jingo-ji and the Daigo-ji in the Kyoto region, and the Murō-ji farther south. See also "Fujiwara period."

hidden roof. See *noyane*.

hijiki (肘木; bracket arm): horizontal components of the bracket system placed on the large bearing block and carrying (usually) three small bearing blocks together with which they support the eaves. See plate 17 and also *funa-hijiki* and *sasaguri*.

hip-and-gable roof construction. See *irimoya-zukuri*.

hipped roof construction. See *yosemune-zukuri*.

hisashi (庇, 廂): an enclosed aisle usually one-bay deep along one or more sides of the core of the building (*moya*). Often *hisashi* surround the *moya* on four sides. The roof of the *hisashi* is often of a more gradual slope than that of the *moya*. See plates 6–7, 9.

hokkedō (法華堂; Lotus Sutra hall): the hall of a temple complex which houses the ceremonial reading of the Lotus Sutra; also called *hokke-sammaidō* (法華三昧堂). The most famous *hokkedō* is at Tōdai-ji. See plates 71–73.

irimoya-zukuri (入母屋造; hip-and-gable roof construction): a roof combining a gable roof on the upper part and a hip roof on the lower. The most common roof type for

kondō and lecture halls, the Hōryū-ji *kondō* roof is one example (pl. 39).

kaerumata (蟇股; frog-leg struts): decorative struts of solid wood or later with the center cut out; in either case, they resemble in shape the legs of a crouching frog, hence the name. They are Chinese in origin. Although functional at first, they became, for the most part, strictly decorative from the middle of the Heian period. See plate 12.

kairō (回廊; semienclosed roofed corridor): long roofed aisles, open on the inner side, surrounding the main nucleus or a separate precinct of the monastery. When a semienclosed roofed corridor surrounds the main nucleus, it often serves as a connective passageway between major monastic buildings like the middle gate, belfry, lecture hall, and sutra repository. See plates 36, 43.

Kamakura period (1185–1330): the historical period covering the years of government by military rulers out of the city of Kamakura, fifty-one kilometers southwest of present-day Tokyo. The history of Buddhist architecture covered in this book ends just prior to the beginning of the Kamakura period.

kanjōdō (灌頂堂; purification hall): a hall for ceremonies whose origins stem from the Indian custom of investiture of the king, in which the king's head is baptized from the water of the Four Rivers. In China this ordination or investiture was a Buddhist rite for high personages only. Esoteric Buddhist sects administer it frequently to monks and laymen.

kashira-nuki. See *nuki*.

ken (間; bay): the basic module in temple architecture. A variable unit of measurement based on the distance between the centers of two pillars. See plate 5.

kentozuka (間斗束): an intercolumnar strut capped by a bearing block. One of the earliest forms of beam support, it was later added in spaces too narrow to accommodate a full bracket set or was used in a span where a purlin needed additional support. Intercolumnar bracket complexes begin in the Kamakura period (1185–1330) and are called *tsumegumi* (詰組). See plate 17.

kirizuma-zukuri (切妻造; gabled roof construction): In this simple type of roof, with two canted sides, front and back, sloping diagonally downward away from the ridge, a gable is formed on each end of the building. This roof style is used in the simplest Chinese and Japanese buildings. The underside of the roof may be visible from the inside of the structure.

kōdō (講堂; lecture hall): a monastery structure where monks and students gather for instruction, reading of texts, ceremonies of repentence, and other congregational meetings. It is usually prominently located in the center rear of the main monastery nucleus.

kokubun-ji (国分寺; provincial temple): temples established by the central government in the provinces. Beginning in 685, when all the provinces were ordered to erect Buddha altars, the official temples of each province were divided into monks' temples (*kokubun-ji*) and nuns' temples (国分尼寺; *kokubun-ni-ji*), for the purpose of keeping all monasteries under the central authority of the government. In 740 a seven-story pagoda was erected in every province of Japan. State control of religious institutions was strong under Emperor Shōmu (r. 724–749).

kondō (金堂; "golden hall"): part of the nucleus of a Buddhist monastery, intended primarily as the main hall to house statues and paintings of deities serving as the focal point of ceremonial worship there. Often the most imposing of the monastery's buildings, the *kondō* was placed together with the pagoda and both surrounded by a semienclosed roofed corridor in the oldest monastic establishments. See plates 39, 97.

kumimono. See *tokyō*.

kyōzō (経蔵; sutra repository): building where sutras and other religious texts or precious

documents are stored, usually placed symmetrically in relation to the belfry. See plate 89.

lattice window. See *renji mado*.

lecture hall. See *kōdō*.

magobisashi (孫庇, 孫廂): a second roofed aisle beyond the front *hisashi*, used as an additional space for the congregation. See plate 8.

makito. See *masu*.

mandokoro (政所): the monastery administrative office, located in the refectory and assembly precinct.

masu or *to* (斗; bearing block): together with the bracket arms, carries the load of the roof and eaves in each bracket set (see *tokyō*). Two main types are the large bearing block (大斗; *daito*), seen as early as the Han dynasty in China (first century A.D.) and the small bearing block (巻斗; *makito*). See plate 17.

middle gate. See *chūmon*.

mokoshi (裳階, 裳層): a one-bay roofed area surrounding a building like a lean-to, originally intended to give added protection to the interior. It usually appears only in Japanese Buddhist architecture. Lodged under the main eaves of a roof, the *mokoshi* often gives the false impression of an extra story. The Hōryū-ji *kondō* and pagoda and the Yakushi-ji east pagoda are the only examples surviving from the ancient period. The *mokoshi* is very common in Zen Buddhist architecture in the medieval period. See plate 10.

Monju hall (文殊堂; *monjudō*): a hall dedicated to, and housing an image of, Monju (Mañjuśrī), the bodhisattva of wisdom.

moya (母屋, 身屋, 身舍): originally the central space of a residential building. The term was taken over in Buddhist architecture to designate the central space under the main roof in which the altar is usually placed. The *moya* is often enclosed by *hisashi*. See plates 5–8.

nandaimon (南大門; great south gate): the first major entrance at the approach to a monastery, leading to the middle gate, 219 and often on the same axis as the lecture hall.

Nara period. See "Hakuhō period" and "Tempyō period."

noyane (野屋根; hidden roof): the "hidden" roof of the double-roof system characteristic of middle to late Heian Buddhist halls and later the most common roof structure. Beneath it is installed a "visible" roof (化粧屋根; *keshōyane*), the rafters of which are of different slope and which conceal the hidden roof's supporting timbers underneath. Each roof of the double roof system has an independent support structure. See plates 16, 158.

nuki (貫; penetrating tie-beam): a general term for a horizontal penetrating tie-beam which extends from pillar to pillar. In the ancient period, head tie-beams (頭貫; *kashira-nuki*), which were inserted into the tops of the pillars, were the only penetrating tie-beams used. After the introduction of new styles from China, beginning in the thirteenth century, other penetrating tie-beams came into use, for example, at the center of the pillar shaft or at the base. See plates 3, 17, 19.

odaruki (尾垂木; "tail" rafter): a long lever arm whose outer end bears the weight of the eaves overhang, and whose inner end is anchored into the framework above the interior columns. It existed in Chinese architecture probably from the Northern Wei dynasty (early sixth century) and in Japan since the Asuka period. See plate 17.

raidō (礼堂): a prayer or worship hall. Originally a free-standing hall for public worship, it was joined to the main hall to form a single structure in the Heian period.

renji mado (連子窓; lattice window): a mullioned window fitted with rows of thin wooden bars set vertically in the opening. Such windows can be seen in plate 89.

Shaka hall. See *shakadō*.

sasaguri (笹繰): the scoop of a bracket arm. This scoop appears in Northern Wei, early T'ang, and Asuka-period architecture, but it is lost by the time of the Tōshōdai-ji.

See plate 17.

semienclosed roofed corridor. See *kairō*.

shakadō (釈迦堂; Śākyamuni hall): a hall dedicated to, and housing an image of, the Śākyamuni Buddha.

shaku (尺): a unit of linear measurement originating in China and employed in Korea and Japan. Varying in its length, during the Tempyō period and in T'ang China it was approximately thirty centimeters long.

shirin (支輪): curved struts which form a transition between wall and ceiling. See plate 17.

Shōmu, Emperor (701–756): the Japanese emperor during whose reign (724–749) Buddhism flourished, and under whose patronage much of Tōdai-ji, including the Great Buddha (Daibutsu), was built. During his reign, too, a survey was made of all the provinces in Japan, and official examinations for public office, in imitation of the Chinese system, were first held. Emperor Shōmu reigned twenty-five years and then abdicated in favor of his daughter, who became the empress Kōken. He took the tonsure and lived seven more years.

Shōtoku, Prince (Shōtoku Taishi, 572–621): prince-regent and nephew of Empress Suiko, credited with the propagation of Buddhist ethics in Japan during the reign of his aunt, from the last decade of the sixth century until his death. Prince Shōtoku patronized the construction of many Buddhist monasteries, including the Shitennō-ji and Hōryū-ji, and encouraged Korean and Chinese specialists in religion, scholarship, and the arts to come and settle in his country.

shurō or *shōrō* (鐘楼; belfry): a two-story structure which houses the bell of a monastery in its upper story. It is often built opposite the sutra repository. See plate 178.

strut. See *tsuka*.

sutra repository. See *kyōzō*.

tail rafter. See *odaruki*.

Tempyō period (711–781): the late Nara period, named after the second regnal era (729–749) of Emperor Shōmu, one of the greatest patrons of Buddhist art and architecture in Japan. The period includes most of the major monastery projects of Nara, including Tōdai-ji, Yakushi-ji, and Tōshōdai-ji. This period was one of great absorption of Chinese manners and taste, well represented in the capital of Heijō.

tie-beam. See *nuki*.

tokyō (斗栱) or *kumimono* (組物; bracket system): a type of corbelled roof support using bracket sets, one of the distinctive features of Chinese and Japanese architecture. Based on the principle of a kind of cantilevered support, it underwent considerable technical and stylistic elaboration in both China and Japan. It projects purlin-carrying bracket arms outward in steps and upward in tiers. See plate 17. See also *hijiki* and *masu*.

tsuka (束; strut): a simple vertical strut, short post, or prop. See also *kentozuka*.

worship hall. See *raidō*.

yakushidō (薬師堂): a hall dedicated to, and housing an image of, Yakushi (Bhaiṣajya-guru), the Buddha of healing.

yosemune-zukuri (寄棟造; hipped roof construction): a roof with canted ridges sloping away from the main ridge. In Chinese usage, this was the most symmetrical and hence ideal roof type, reserved for the most monumental and highest-rank buildings. In Japan greater preference was given to the hip-and-gable roof (*irimoya-zukuri*). An example is the Tōshōdai-ji *kondō* (pl. 97).

BIBLIOGRAPHY

JAPANESE SOURCES
(compiled and annotated by the author)

足立　康　『飛鳥奈良時代の仏教建築』（岩波講座）　東京　岩波書店　昭和 8 年　[Adachi, Kō. *Buddhist Architecture of the Asuka and Nara Periods*. Iwanami Lectures on Japanese History. Tokyo: Iwanami Shoten, 1933].
　　One of the earliest systematic accounts of the architectural history of these periods to be based on extant structures and the differences in monastery plans.

——— 『薬師寺伽藍の研究』（日本古文化研究所報告 5 ）　昭和12年　[———. *A Study of the Yakushi-ji Monastery*. Bulletin of the Center for the Study of Early Japanese Culture, no. 5, 1937].
　　Presents the thesis that the Yakushi-ji built in the Heijō capital (about 718) was an exact copy of the original Yakushi-ji at the Fujiwara capital (built 687) and therefore the still extant east pagoda of the later Yakushi-ji is in the architectural style of the late seventh century.

浅野　清　『法隆寺建築綜観』　京都　便利堂　昭和28年　[Asano, Kiyoshi. *A Comprehensive View of Hōryū-ji Architecture*. Kyoto: Benridō, 1953].
　　On the basis of the results of the repair work in which he participated at the Hōryū-ji, the author throws light on the original design and building techniques of various structures of the Hōryū-ji.

——— 『奈良時代建築の研究』　東京　中央公論美術出版　昭和44年　[———. *A Study of Nara-Period Architecture*. Tokyo: Chūō Kōron Bijutsu Shuppan, 1969].
　　An examination of extant structures from the eighth century and a reconstruction of their original appearance, with particularly detailed treatment given to Hōryū-ji's Dempō-dō.

浅野　清・毛利　久　『奈良の寺院と天平彫刻』（原色日本の美術 3 ）　東京　小学館　昭和41年　[Asano, Kiyoshi, and Mōri, Hisashi. *Nara Monasteries and Tempyō Sculpture*. Japanese Art in Color, vol. 3. Tokyo: Shōgakkan, 1966].
　　The architectural section of this book, presenting a discussion of eighth-century temple design and structure, is notable for its detailed commentary on structural technique.

浅野　清・鈴木嘉吉　『奈良時代僧房の研究』　奈良国立文化財研究所学報第 4 冊　昭和32年　[Asano, Kiyoshi, and Suzuki, Kakichi. *A Study of Nara-Period Monks' Dormitories*. Research Report of the Nara National Research Institute of Cultural Properties, no. 4, 1957].
　　A monograph which clarified the condition of monks' dormitories of the seventh and eighth centuries, based on a study of the original plans and forms of extant structures as determined during dismantling and repair and a comparison with excavation reports of dormitory sites.

浅野　清他編　『日本 IV 』（世界考古学大系 4 ）　東京　平凡社　昭和36年　[Asano, Kiyoshi *et al.*, eds.

Japan IV. Outline of World Archaeology, vol. 4. Tokyo: Heibonsha, 1961].
The chapter ''Buried Temples'' (埋もれた寺院) contains a description of the characteristics of temple architecture in the seventh and eighth centuries, based on the results
of excavations at numerous temple sites carried out during the 1950s.

福山敏男 『天台真言宗の建築』 東京 雄山閣 昭和11年 [Fukuyama, Toshio. *Architecture of the
Tendai and Shingon Sects*. Lectures on Buddhist Archaeology. Tokyo: Yūzankaku, 1936].
Architecture of the Tendai and Shingon sects commenced in the early Heian period,
but none of the buildings of that time have survived. This work, based on documentary
evidence, shed light on their appearance.

———. 『日本建築史の研究』 東京 桑名文星堂 昭和18年 [———. *A Study of Japanese Architectural History*. Tokyo: Kuwanabunseidō, 1943].
A collection of articles on the chronology and architectural characteristics of ancient
temples and shrines, one of which revealed the process of constructing Buddha halls
(*butsudō*) in the Nara period, based on documents in the Shōsō-in, and was a ground-
breaking study.

———. 『奈良朝寺院の研究』 高桐書院 昭和23年 [———. *A Study of Nara-Period Monasteries*.
Takagiri Shoin, 1948].
A compilation of the names and histories of monasteries built in the Nara period, based
on documentary evidence.

———. 『薬師寺』 東京 東京大学出版会 昭和33年 [———. *The Yakushi-ji*. Tokyo: Tokyo University Press, 1958].
A detailed study of the history and architecture of the Yakushi-ji.

———. 『平等院と中尊寺』 (日本の美術9) 東京 平凡社 昭和39年 [———. *Byōdō-in and Chūson-
ji*. Japanese Arts, vol. 9. Tokyo: Heibonsha, 1964. For English translation, see ''Further
Reading''].

Describes temple architecture at the end of the ancient period, focusing on the Byōdō-
in and Chūson-ji as representative examples of the new monastery plans and Amida
hall architecture that arose with the popularity of the Pure Land sect from the eleventh
century onward.

———. 『日本建築史研究』 東京 墨水書房 昭和43年 [———. *A Study in Japanese Architectural
History*. Tokyo: Bokusui Shobō, 1968].
A collection of papers on ancient shrine and temple architecture, with the discussion
of the Shōsō-in and the various storehouses at Tōdai-ji being particularly detailed.

石田茂作 『総説飛鳥時代寺院址の研究』 東京 大塚巧藝社 昭和19年 [Ishida, Mosaku. *A Comprehensive Study of Asuka-Period Monastery Sites*. Tokyo: Ōtsuka Kōgeisha, 1944].
An investigation, from old roof tiles, of temple sites thought to have been established
from the end of the sixth century to around the middle of the seventh, with a discussion
of monastery plans and characteristics at about fifty locations throughout the country.

———. 『伽藍論攷』 奈良県 天理市 養徳社 昭和23年 [———. *Monastery Assessments*. Nara Pref.:
Tenri City, 1948].
Sequel to *A Comprehensive Study of Asuka-Period Monastery Sites*, this book is chiefly the
record of the characteristics of seventh-century monastery plans. Excavation reports

223

from the Wakakusa-dera and contemporaneous Korean monasteries are included.

伊東忠太 『日本建築の研究』 東京 竜吟社 昭和17年 [Itō, Chūta. *A Study of Japanese Architecture.* Tokyo: Ryūginsha, 1942].

A collection of papers on the stylistic history of Japanese architecture from the Hōryū-ji on.

三上次男・楢崎彰一編『歴史時代 下』（日本の考古学7） 東京 河出書房 昭和42年 [Mikami, Tsugio, and Narasaki, Shōichi, eds. *The Historical Age*, part 2. Japanese Archaeology, vol. 7. Tokyo: Kawade Shobō, 1967].

The section "Buddhist Temples" （寺院） contains an account of architectural characteristics of ancient temples as revealed in site excavations.

大岡 実『奈良の寺』（日本の美術7） 東京 平凡社 昭和40年 [Ōoka, Minoru. *The Temples of Nara.* Japanese Arts, vol. 7. Tokyo: Heibonsha, 1965. For English translation, see "Further Reading"].

A discussion of the architectural characteristics of the so-called seven great temples of Nara, including the Kōfuku-ji, Yakushi-ji, and Tōshōdai-ji, built at the Heijō capital in the eighth century.

―――― 『南都七大寺の研究』 東京 中央公論美術出版 昭和41年 [――――. *A Study of the Seven Great Temples of the Southern Capital.* Tokyo: Chūō Kōron Bijutsu Shuppan, 1966].

A collection of papers published between 1928 and 1965 describing the monastery plans and characteristics of the so-called seven great temples of Nara, based on the results of detailed measurements.

太田博太郎 『法隆寺建築』 東京 彰国社 昭和18年 [Ōta, Hirotarō. *Architecture of the Hōryū-ji.* Tokyo: Shōkokusha, 1943].

A detailed account of the monastery plan and architectural history of the Hōryū-ji.

―――― 『日本建築史序説』 東京 彰国社 昭和22年 [――――. *An Introduction to the History of Japanese Architecture.* Tokyo: Shōkokusha, 1947].

An overview of Japanese architecture from ancient times to the nineteenth century. Clear discussion of the special features of each age, examining the connections between the evolutions of Buddhist monasteries, Shinto shrines, residential dwellings, and castle architecture.

太田博太郎・福山敏男 『日本建築史』 （建築学大系4） 東京 彰国社 昭和32年 [Ōta, Hirotarō, and Fukuyama, Toshio. *Japanese Architectural History.* An Outline of Architecture, vol. 4. Tokyo: Shōkokusha, 1957].

A historical survey of Japanese architecture divided into early, medieval, and recent (up to nineteenth century) periods, constituting the best summation of research results up to that time.

太田博太郎他 『日本・古代』 （世界建築全集1） 東京 平凡社 昭和36年 [Ōta, Hirotarō *et al. Japan: The Ancient Period.* Collected World Architecture, vol. 1. Tokyo: Heibonsha, 1961].

A concise history of ancient Japanese architecture.

太田博太郎他 『奈良六大寺大観』 全14巻 東京 岩波書店 昭和43〜48年 [Ōta, Hirotarō *et al. Survey of the Six Great Temples of Nara.* 14 vols. Tokyo: Iwanami Shoten, 1968–73].

A profusely illustrated, detailed, multivolume study of the architecture, sculpture, and other features of the Hōryū-ji, Yakushi-ji, Kōfuku-ji, Tōdai-ji, Tōshōdai-ji, and Saidai-ji, constituting the best summation of recent research.

太田博太郎他 『大和古寺大観』 全7巻 東京 岩波書店 昭和49〜53年 [Ōta, Hirotarō *et al. Survey of the Ancient Temples of Yamato.* 7 vols. Tokyo: Iwanami Shoten, 1974–78].
Multivolume survey of the architecture and sculpture of monasteries of the Nara region not covered in the *Survey of the Six Great Temples of Nara,* including the Hokki-ji, Gangō-ji, and Taima-dera.

関野 貞 『日本の建築と芸術』 東京 岩波書店 昭和15年 [Sekino, Tadasu. *Japanese Architecture and Art.* Tokyo: Iwanami Shoten, 1940].
A collection of various papers published by the writer prior to 1935, among which those on the chronology and history of roof tiles are most detailed.

杉山信三 『藤原氏の氏寺と院家』 奈良国立文化財研究所学報 第19冊 昭和43年 [Sugiyama, Shinzō. *Fujiwara Family Temples and Their Residential Precincts.* Research Report of the Nara National Research Institute of Cultural Properties, no. 19, 1968].
A discussion of the close relationship between temples and aristocratic residential architecture at the end of the ancient period; based on a study of documents and sites of temples erected by the Fujiwara family, who played a central role in aristocratic rule beginning at the end of the tenth century.

田中重久 『奈良朝以前寺院趾の考古学的研究』 東京 東京考古学会 昭和16年 [Tanaka, Shigehisa. *An Archaeological Study of Pre-Nara-Period Monastery Sites.* Tokyo: Tokyo Institute of Archaeology, 1941].
Mainly a comparative study of seventh-century monastery remains and a classification of monastery plan types.

Repair and Restoration Reports

The repairing of structures designated by the government as being of special cultural value began in Japan in 1897, and to date the reparation of about 2,000 structures has been completed. In the reparation of wooden structures, the entire building is dismantled down to the foundation stones, and the rebuilding generally follows the same steps as at the time of original construction, making it a thorough enterprise. The building is meticulously examined during this process, areas that have been repaired or rebuilt by later generations are restored, and a study of the methods of construction used in the original building is carried out. The results are published in a report (修理工事報告書, *shūri kōji hōkokusho*) after the restoration process has been completed. The report consists of photographs and diagrams of the building before and after restoration as well as photographs taken and findings made during the restoration process. The scholarly level of the report, which covers several hundred pages, is very high. These reports, which have appeared in published form since the 1930s, now number some 900; below are listed those that deal with structures from the ancient period. Copies of these reports, limited in number, are distributed to Japanese national libraries and the architecture departments of the major Japanese universities.

The Hōryū-ji great east gate	1935
The Hōryū-ji refectory (*jikidō*)	1936

The Hōryū-ji Daikōdō	1941
The Hōryū-ji east precinct Yumedono	1943
The Hōryū-ji Dempō-dō	1943
The Yakushi-ji east pagoda	1952
The Hōryū-ji five-story pagoda	1955
The Hōryū-ji *kondō*	1956
The Ganjō-ji (Shiramizu) Amida hall	1956
The Gangō-ji Gokuraku-bō main hall (*hondō*) and Zenshitsu	1948
The Tamukeyama Shrine treasure hall (*hōko*)	1958
The Hōryū-ji Higashi-muro	1959
The Hōryū-ji Tsuma-muro	1960
The Taima-dera Mandara-dō	1960
The Daigo-ji five-story pagoda	1960
The Ishiyama-dera main hall (*hondō*)	1961
The Tōshōdai-ji treasure hall (*hōzō*) and sutra repository (*kyōzō*)	1962
The Tōdai-ji Hokke-dō sutra repository (*kyōko*)	1964
The Hōryū-ji Kōfū-zō	1966
The Kairyūō-ji west *kondō*	1967
The Jōruri-ji main hall (*hondō*)	1967
The Gangō-ji Gokuraku-bō miniature pagoda (*shōtō*)	1968
The Chūson-ji Konjiki-dō	1970
The Tōshōdai-ji lecture hall (*kōdō*)	1972
The Hokki-ji three-story pagoda	1976

Excavation Reports

Large-scale excavations of temple sites have been undertaken since around 1955; reports (発掘調査報告書; *hakkutsu chōsa hōkokusho*) on the following have been published in book form.

Asuka-dera
Kawara-dera
Hōryū-ji east precinct (*tōin*)
Shitennō-ji
Kōfuku-ji refectory (*jikidō*)
Mutsu Kokubun-ji (Miyagi Pref.)
Tagajō Takasaki-dera ruins (Miyagi Pref.)
Tōtōmi Kokubun-ji (Shizuoka Pref.)
Settsu Itami-dera (Hyōgo Pref.)
Mōtsu-ji
Muryōkō-in ruins (Iwate Pref.)

FURTHER READING
(selected and annotated by Nancy Shatzman Steinhardt)

de Visser, M. W. *Ancient Buddhism in Japan*. 2 vols. Leiden: E. J. Brill, 1935.
A chronological compilation of Buddhist ceremonies performed in the first five centuries of Japanese Buddhism as they are described in contemporaneous documents.

Fukuyama Toshio. *Heian Temples: Byodo-in and Chuson-ji*. Translated by Richard L. Gage. Heibonsha Survey of Japanese Art, vol. 9. New York and Tokyo: Weatherhill and Heibonsha, 1976.
Survey of the eleventh and twelfth century halls and images dedicated to Amida (Amitābha) Buddha, and related building projects throughout Japan.

Futagawa, Yukio. "The Hall of the Great Buddha at Tōdaiji." *The Japan Architect*, June 1964, p. 47.
Illustrations of the framework of walls and ceiling with short descriptive text.

Hakeda, Yoshito. *Kukai: Major Works, Translated with an Account of His Life and a Study of His Thought*. New York: Columbia University Press. 1972.
Excellent account of the life of the transmitter of Shingon Buddhism to Japan and his role in the transformation of Buddhism in the early Heian period, including translations of many of his most important writings.

Hall, John Whitney. *Japan: From Prehistory to Modern Times*. New York: Dell, 1970.
A clear survey of Japanese political history from its beginnings to the twentieth century.

Higuchi, Kiyoshi. "The Tōshōdaiji." *The Japan Architect*, June 1964, p. 75.
Very general article about the Tōshōdai-ji; good photographs.

Ito, Nobuo. "The Hōryūji Temple." *The Japan Architect*, May 1961, pp. 8–13.
Presentation of some of the most recent findings on the Hōryū-ji, including a discussion of its building date.

———. "The Styles of Japanese Architecture." *The Japan Architect*, June 1964, p. 69.
A definition of the Japanese aesthetic which includes native Japanese shrines, Chinese influence, and the Buddhist style in Japan.

Kidder, J. Edward. *Japanese Temples*. London: Thames and Hudson, 1964.
A profusely illustrated survey of the major Buddhist temples in Japan.

———. *Early Buddhist Japan*. New York: Praeger, 1972.
A cultural and artistic history of Japan to the Heian period, using data from excavations and archaeology reports.

Kobayashi, Takeshi. *Nara Buddhist Art: Todai-ji*. Translated by Richard L. Gage. Heibonsha Survey of Japanese Art, vol. 5. New York and Tokyo: Weatherhill and Heibonsha, 1975.
A discussion of the sculpture of one of the largest monasteries in Japan in the context of Nara Buddhism.

Machida, K. "A Historical Survey of the Controversy as to Whether the Hōryū-ji Was Rebuilt or Not." *Acta Asiatica* 15 (1968) 87–115.
Presentation of the various scholarly viewpoints on the Hōryū-ji fire of 670 in an attempt to prove that the Wakakusa-dera did burn and the present Hōryū-ji was built anew in the early Hakuhō period.

Mizuno, Seiichi. *Asuka Buddhist Art: Horyu-ji*. Translated by Richard L. Gage. Heibonsha

Survey of Japanese Art, vol. 4. New York and Tokyo: Weatherhill and Heibonsha, 1974. Discussion mainly of the architecture and sculpture of the Hōryū-ji, their stylistic features, dates, and relation to other monuments.

Murata, Jiro. "The Phoenix Hall at the Byōdōin." *The Japan Architect*, January/February 1962, pp. 122–27; March 1962, pp. 82–89; April 1962, pp. 81–87. Series of articles giving probably the best English account of the building at that time, with excellent diagrams.

————. "The East Pagoda of the Yakushiji Temple." *The Japan Architect*, August 1962, pp. 84–91. Especially good for its explanation of the framework and the finial.

————. "The Main Hall of Tōshōdaiji." *The Japan Architect*, February 1963, pp. 93–99. Puts the hall in its Chinese context and relates it to other Japanese structures.

————. "The Amitābha Hall at Hōkaiji." *The Japan Architect*, May 1963, pp. 105–9; June 1963, pp. 97–103. Practically the only English coverage of a one-bay-square Amida hall. Also explains the roof and bracketing system.

————. "The Five-storied Pagoda at Daigo-ji." *The Japan Architect*, July 1963, pp. 91–97; August 1963, pp. 97–103. Good in conjunction with Murata's article on the Yakushi-ji east pagoda. Gives a historical survey and explanation of the architectural principles.

Ooka, Minoru. *Temples of Nara and Their Art*. Translated by Dennis Lishka. Heibonsha Survey of Japanese Art, vol. 7. New York and Tokyo: Weatherhill and Heibonsha, 1973. Discussion of the great temples of Nara Prefecture from the Asuka period to the Muromachi period, with references to the spread of Nara styles to other areas.

Paine, R. T., and Soper, Alexander. *The Art and Architecture of Japan*. Rev. ed. New York: Penguin, 1975. Survey of Japanese art and architecture from *jōmon* pottery to the influence of Western art in Japan. The architecture section is excellent.

Parent, Mary Neighbour. "A Reconsideration of the Role of Hōrinji in the History of Japanese Architecture." *The Japan Architect*, January 1977, pp. 77–84; February 1977, pp. 73–80; April 1977, pp. 77–84; May 1977, pp. 77–84; June 1977, pp. 77–84; July 1977, pp. 77–84. The most detailed study of this seventh-century temple in English, focusing on the three-story pagoda and with references to Hōrin-ji's relationship to other temples in the Ikaruga district; well illustrated.

Reischauer, R. K. *Early Japanese History*. 2 vols. Princeton: Princeton University, 1937. Historical survey of Japan through the Heian period. Most useful because of its explanatory charts on government and institutions, chronologies, and translations of official and military terminology.

Sadler, A. L. *A Short History of Japanese Architecture*. Sidney and London: Angus and Robertson, 1941. Still one of the few surveys of Japanese architecture from beginning to end, with many drawings.

Sansom, George. *A Short Cultural History of Japan*. Rev. ed. Stanford: Stanford University Press, 1952.

Highly literate survey of Japanese culture, with sections devoted to religion and the arts.

Saunders, E. Dale. *Buddhism in Japan: With an Outline of Its Origins in India*. Philadelphia: University of Pennsylvania Press, 1964.

Explanation of the basic principles of Japanese Buddhist sects in layman's terminology.

Sawa, Takaaki. *Art in Japanese Esoteric Buddhism*. Translated by Richard L. Gage. Heibonsha Survey of Japanese Art, vol. 8. New York and Tokyo: Weatherhill and Heibonsha, 1972.

Discussion of the major monuments, sites, deities, and sculpture of Esoteric Buddhism.

Seckel, Dietrich. *The Art of Buddhism*. New York: Crown, 1964.

Excellent basic survey of the evolution of Buddhist art from India to East Asia, with concentration on a few specific problems.

Soper, Alexander C. *The Evolution of Buddhist Architecture in Japan*. 1942. Reprint. New York: Hacker Art Books, 1979.

Superbly documented discussion of Buddhist architecture in Japan from the Asuka through Edo periods, with significant sections on the influence of Chinese architecture in Japan.

Varley, H. Paul. *Japanese Culture: A Short History*. New York: Praeger, 1973.

This excellent survey of Japanese culture discusses the major artistic achievements with relation to literary and political developments.

Warner, Langdon. *The Enduring Arts of Japan*. 1952. Reprint. New York: Grove Press, 1958.

Beautifully written discussion of the arts of Japan from the author's point of view.

INDEX